This coloring book belongs to ____________

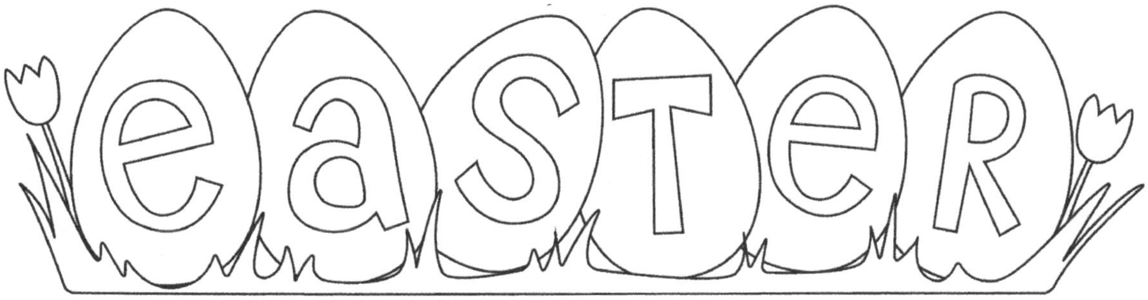

FOR PEEPS SAKE

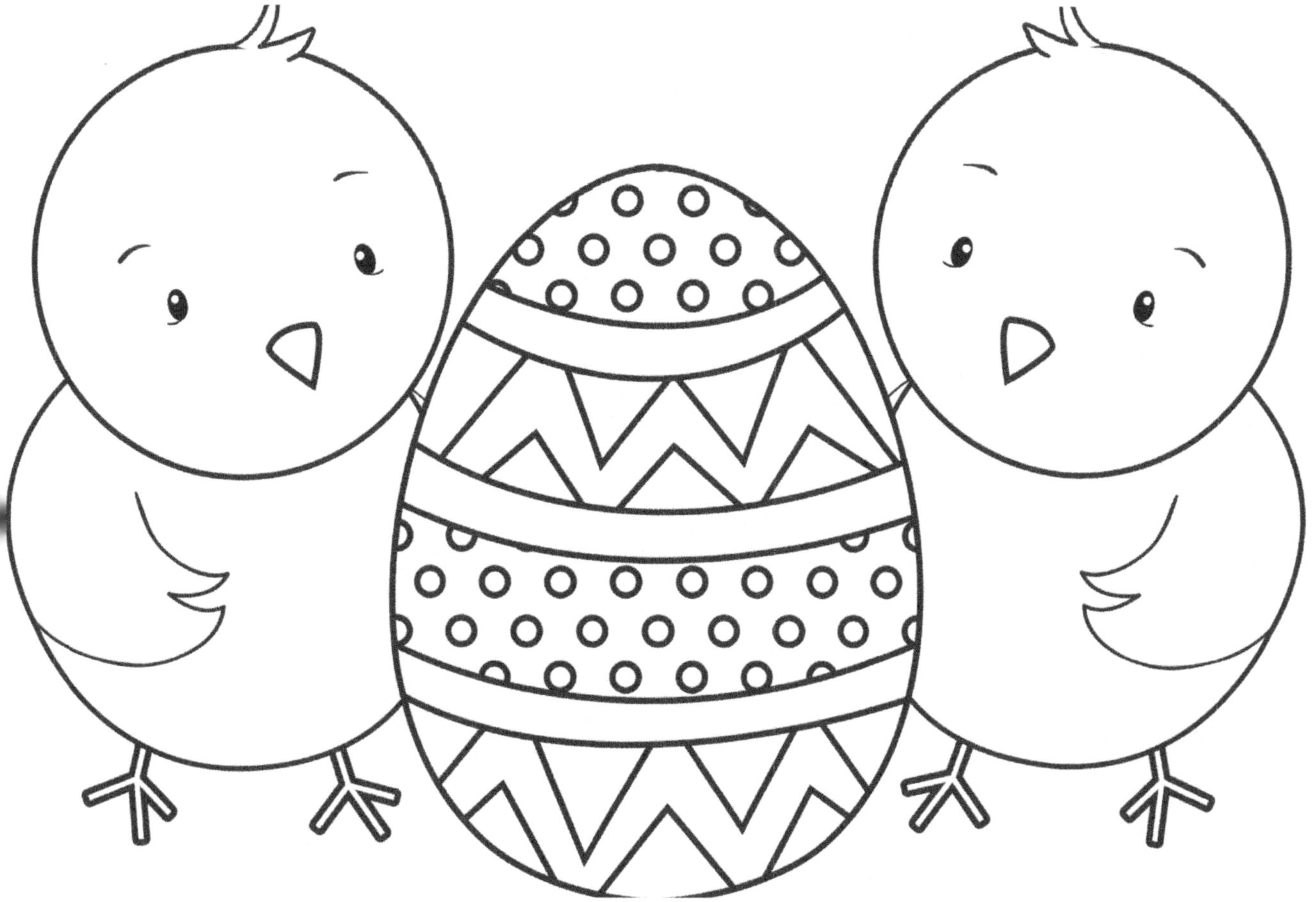

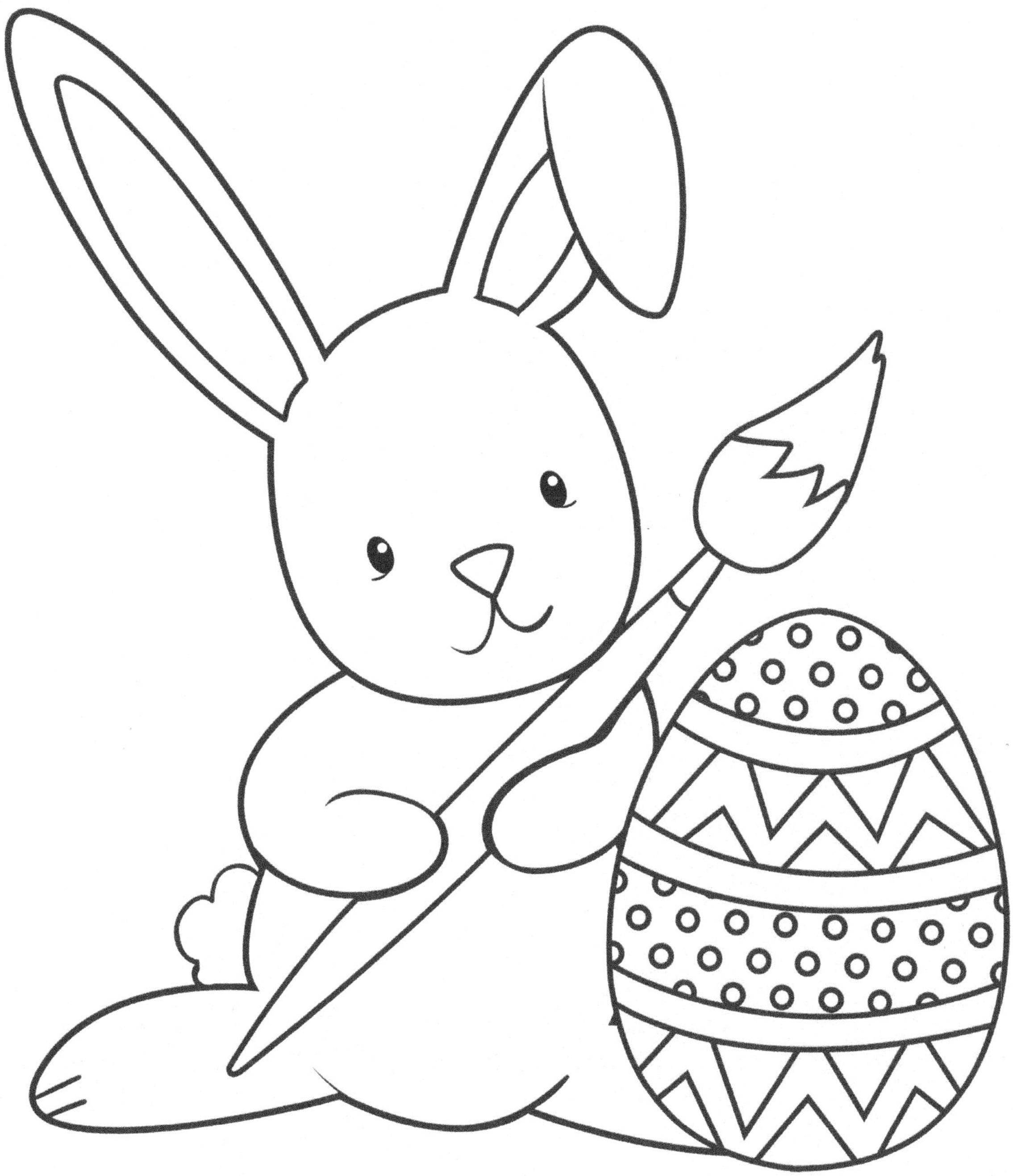

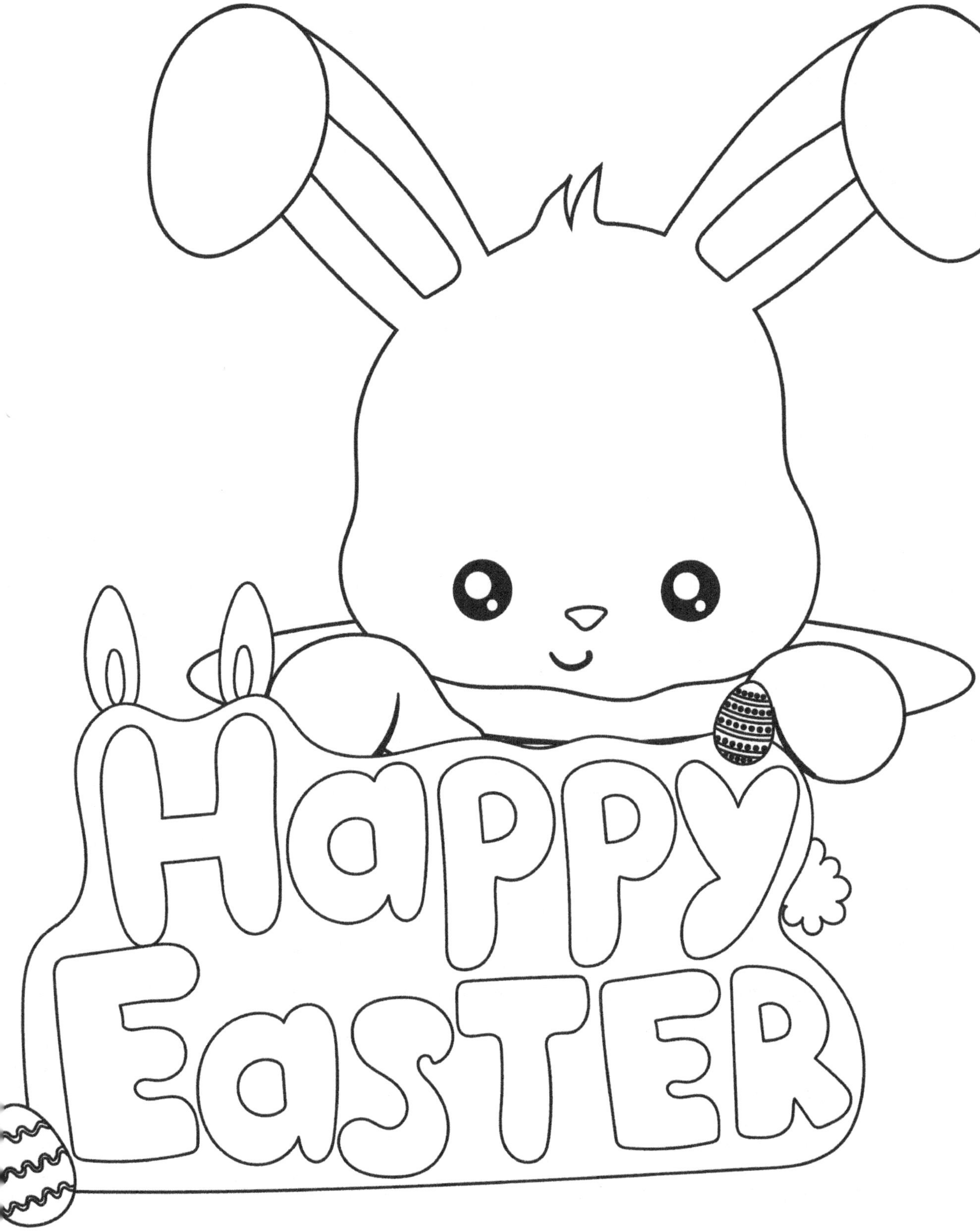
Happy
Easter

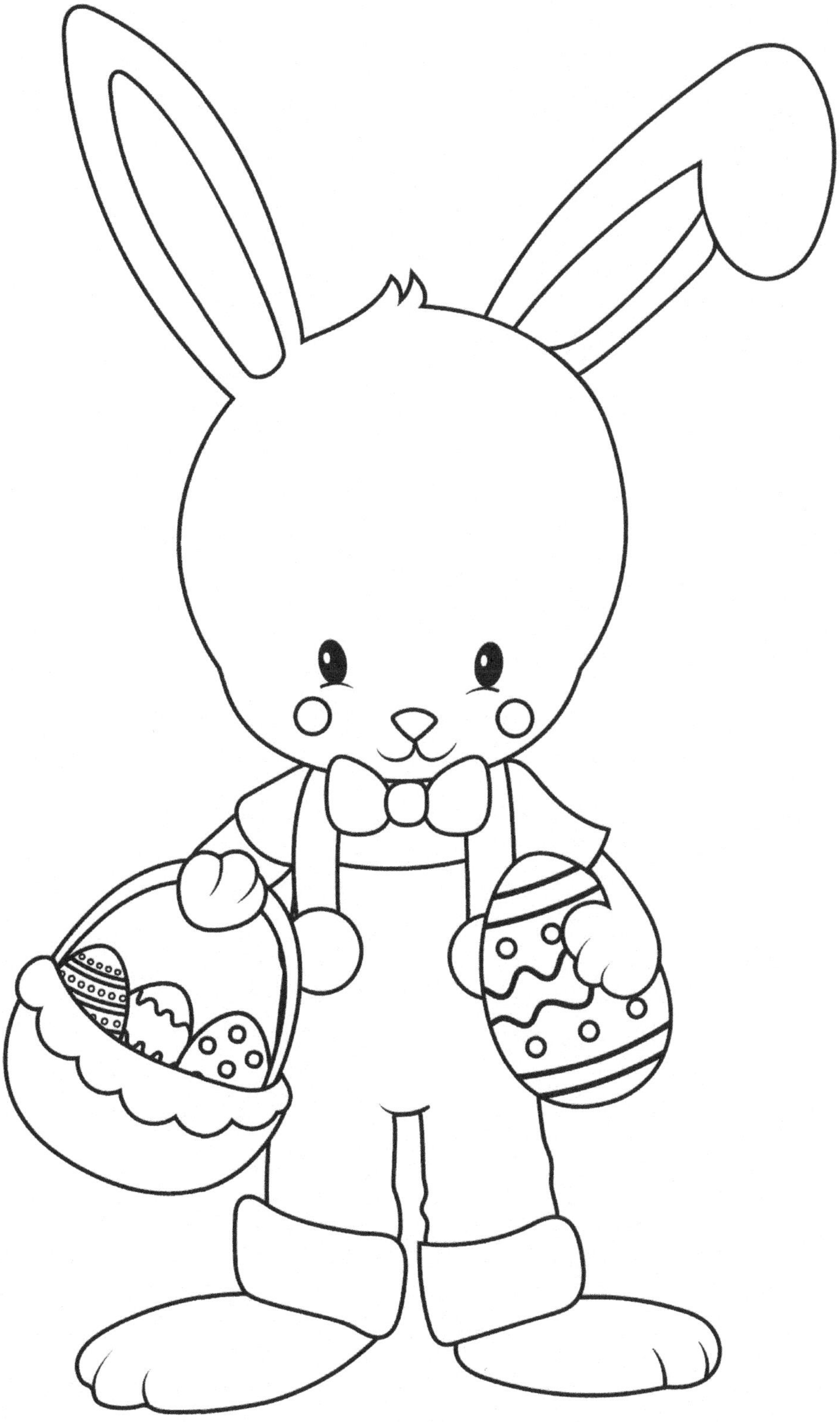

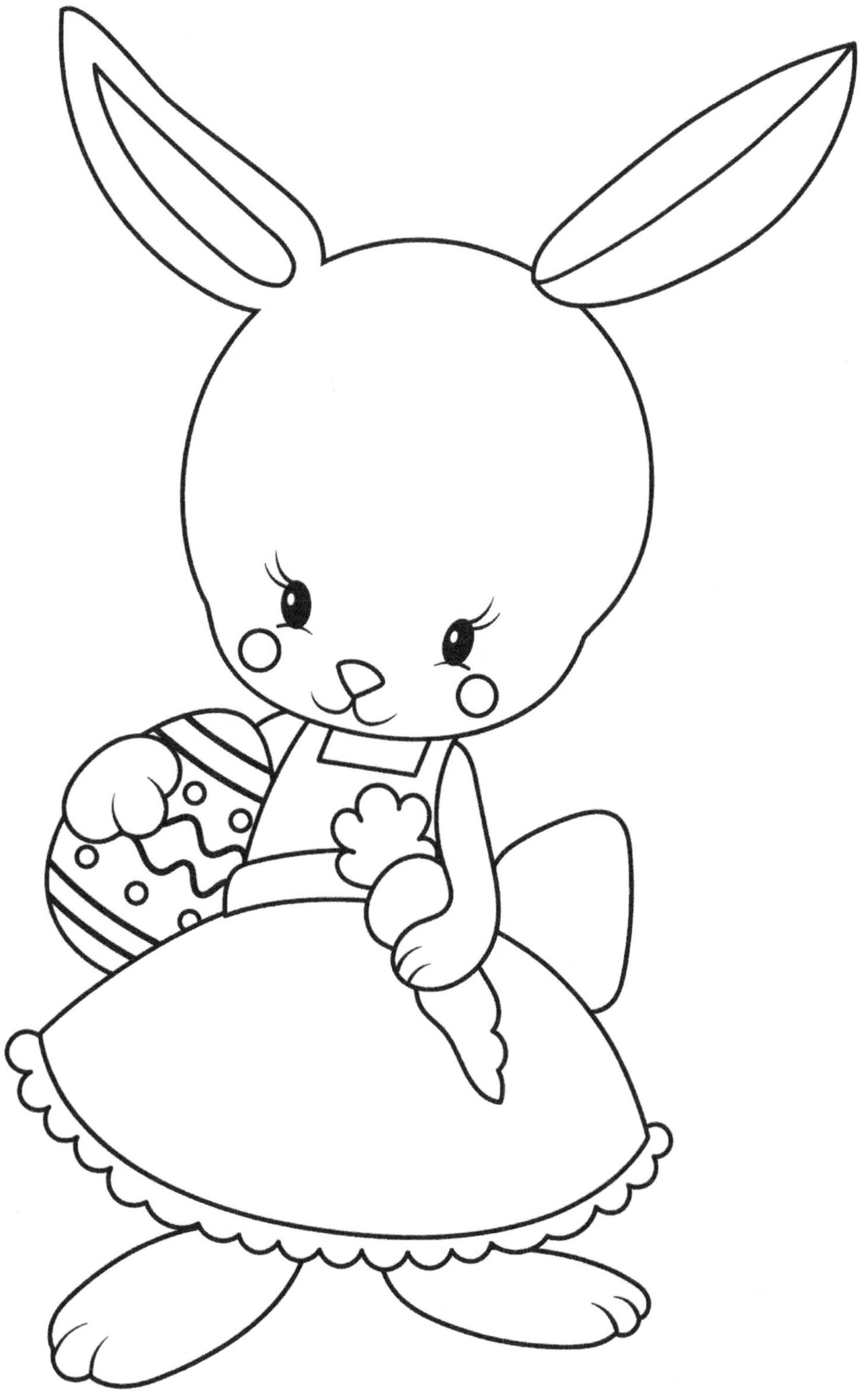

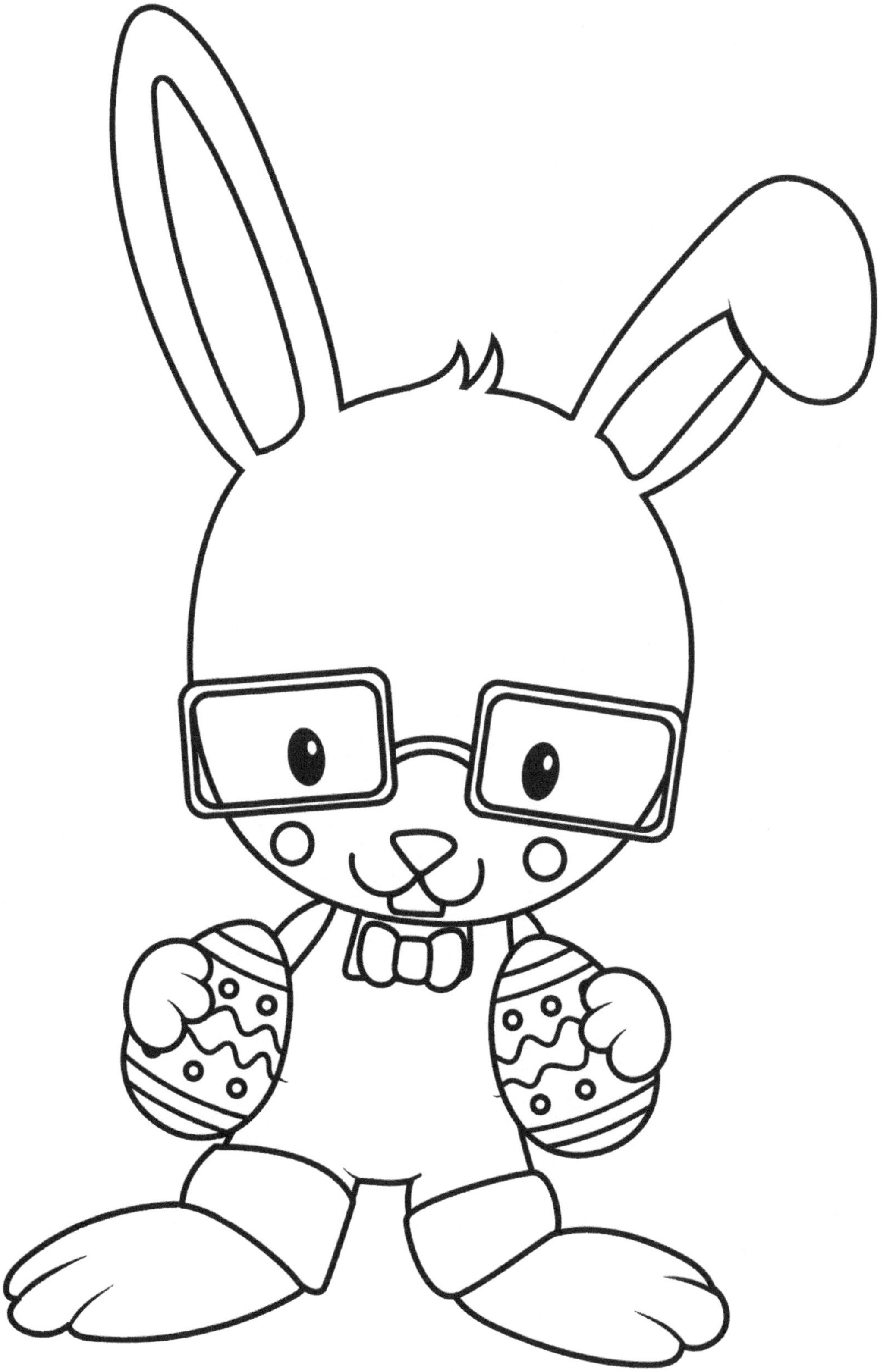

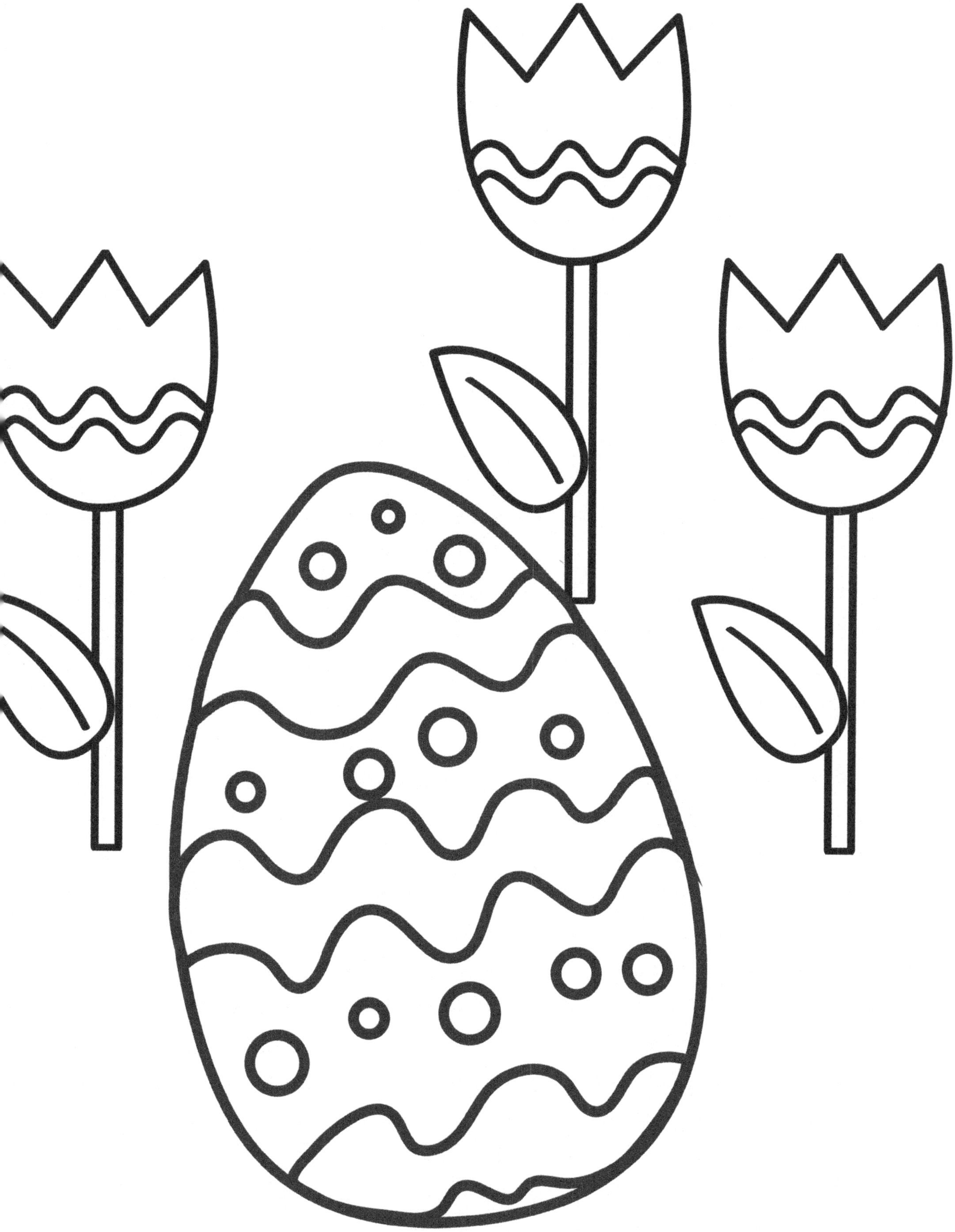

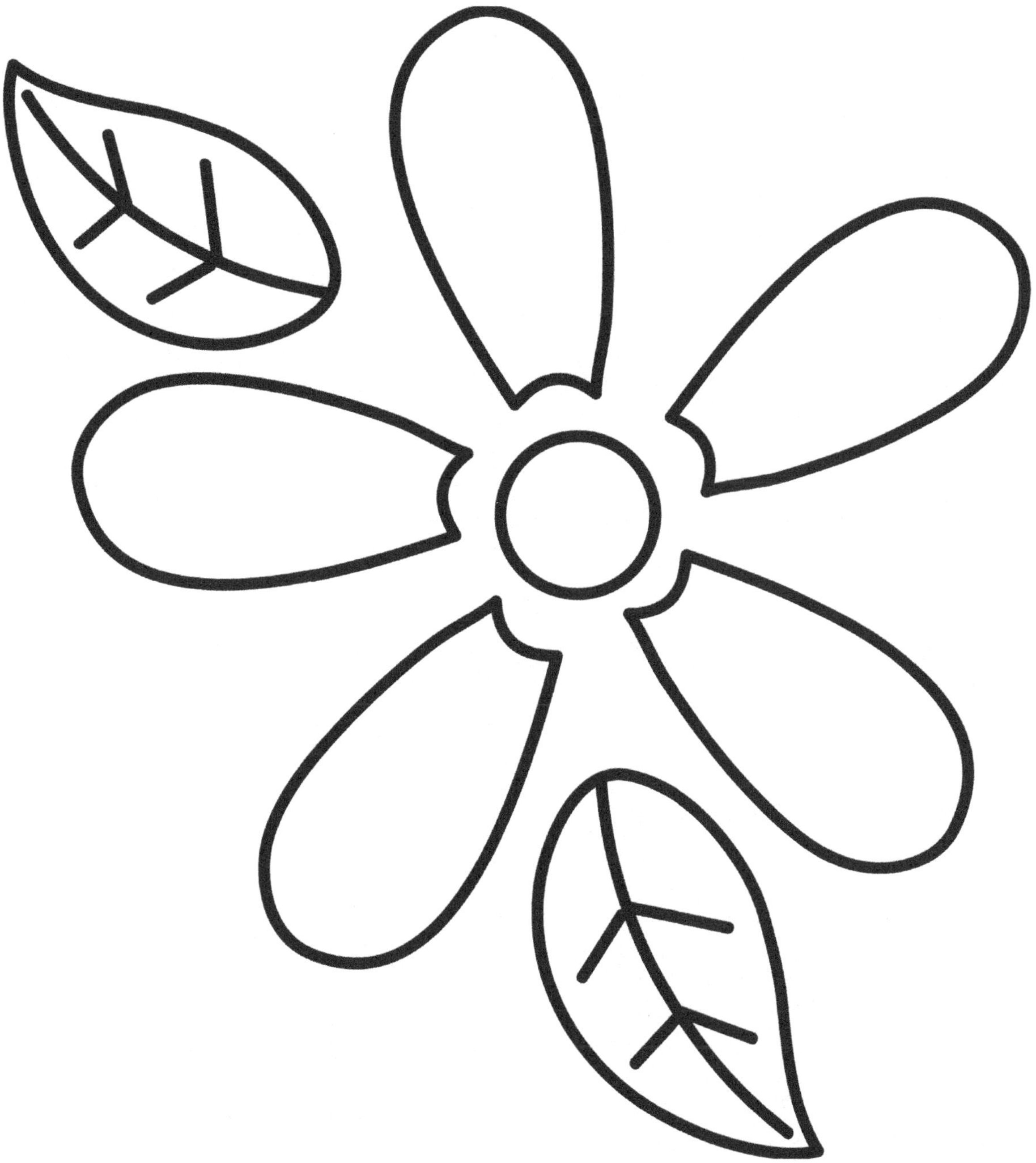

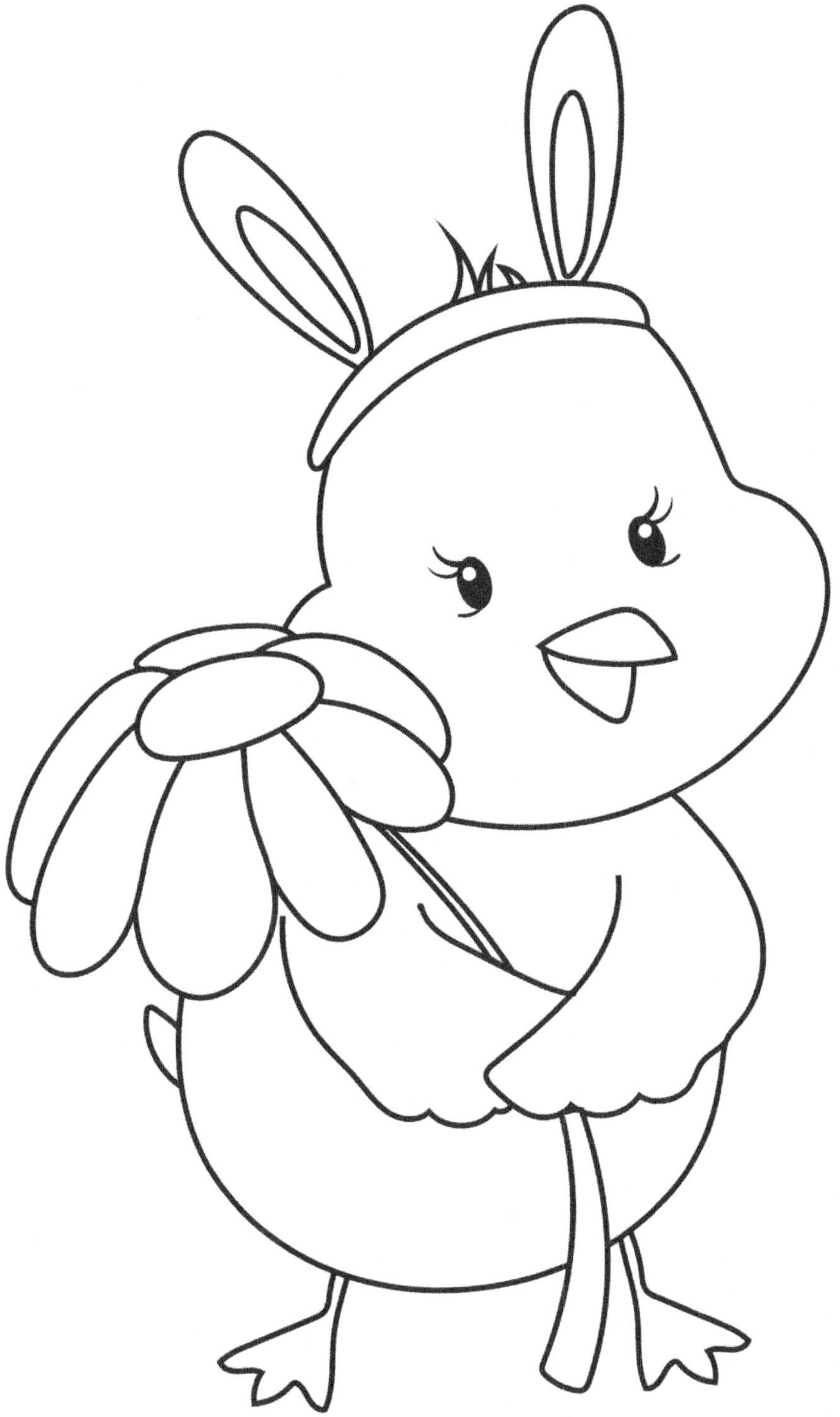

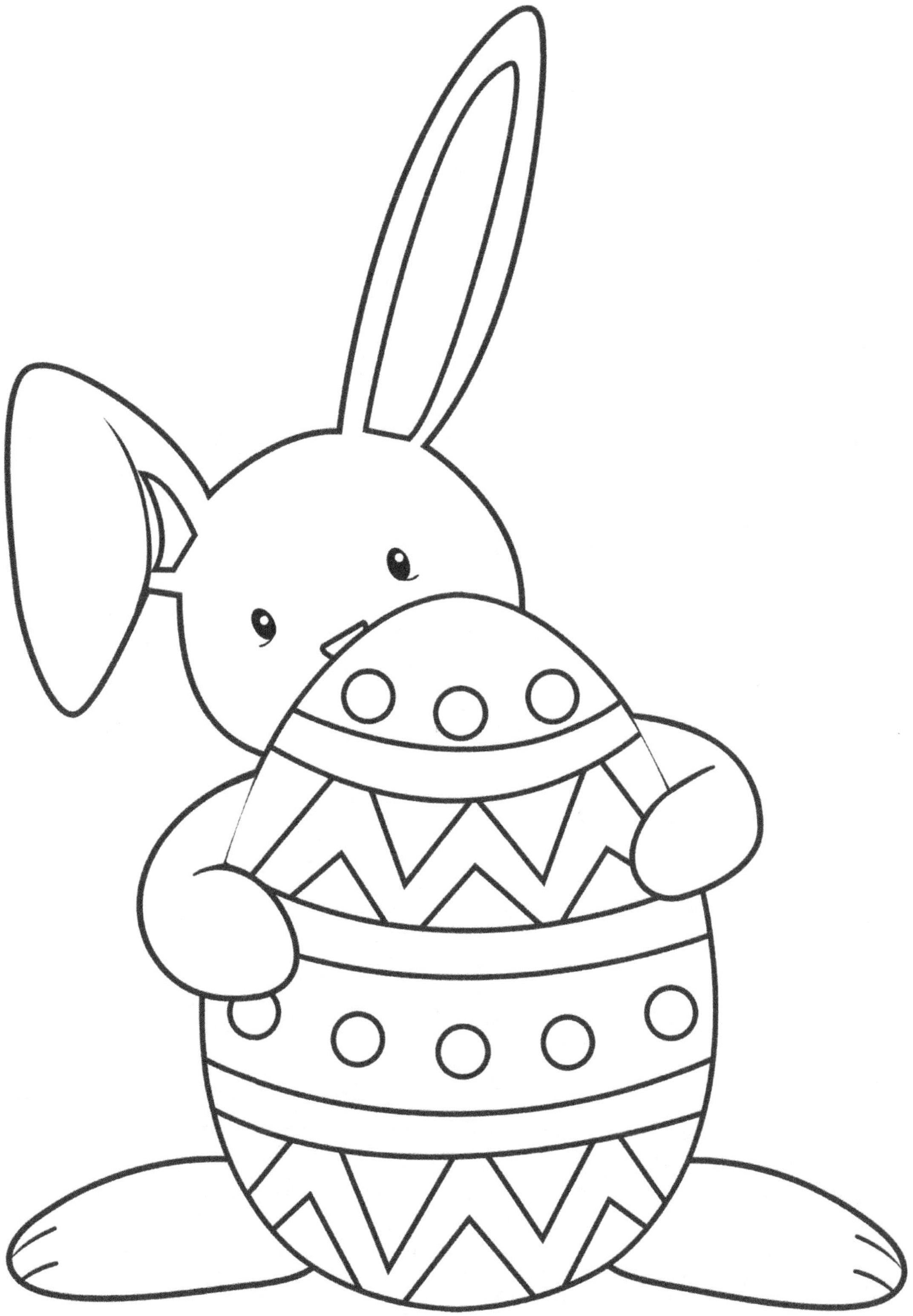

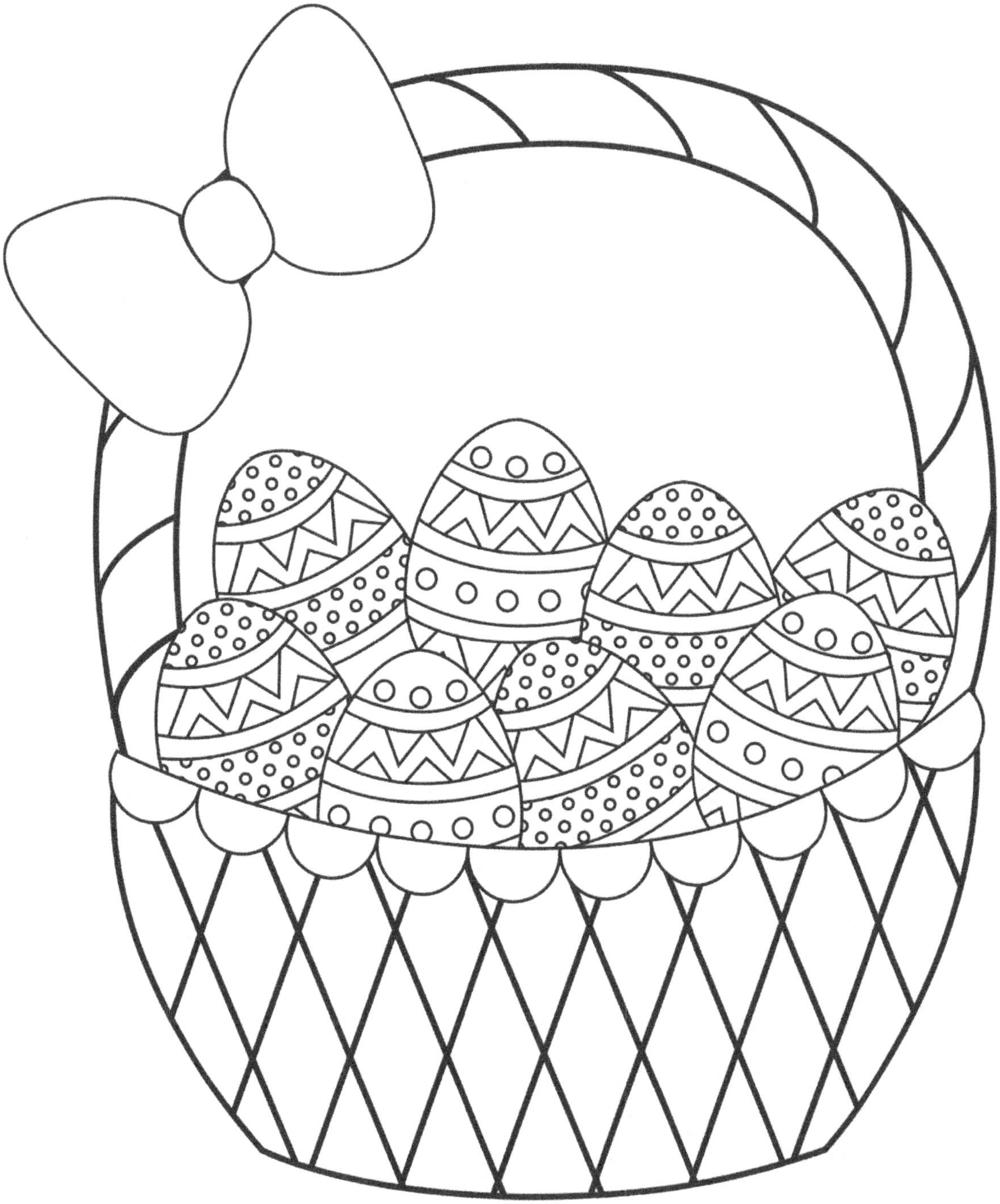

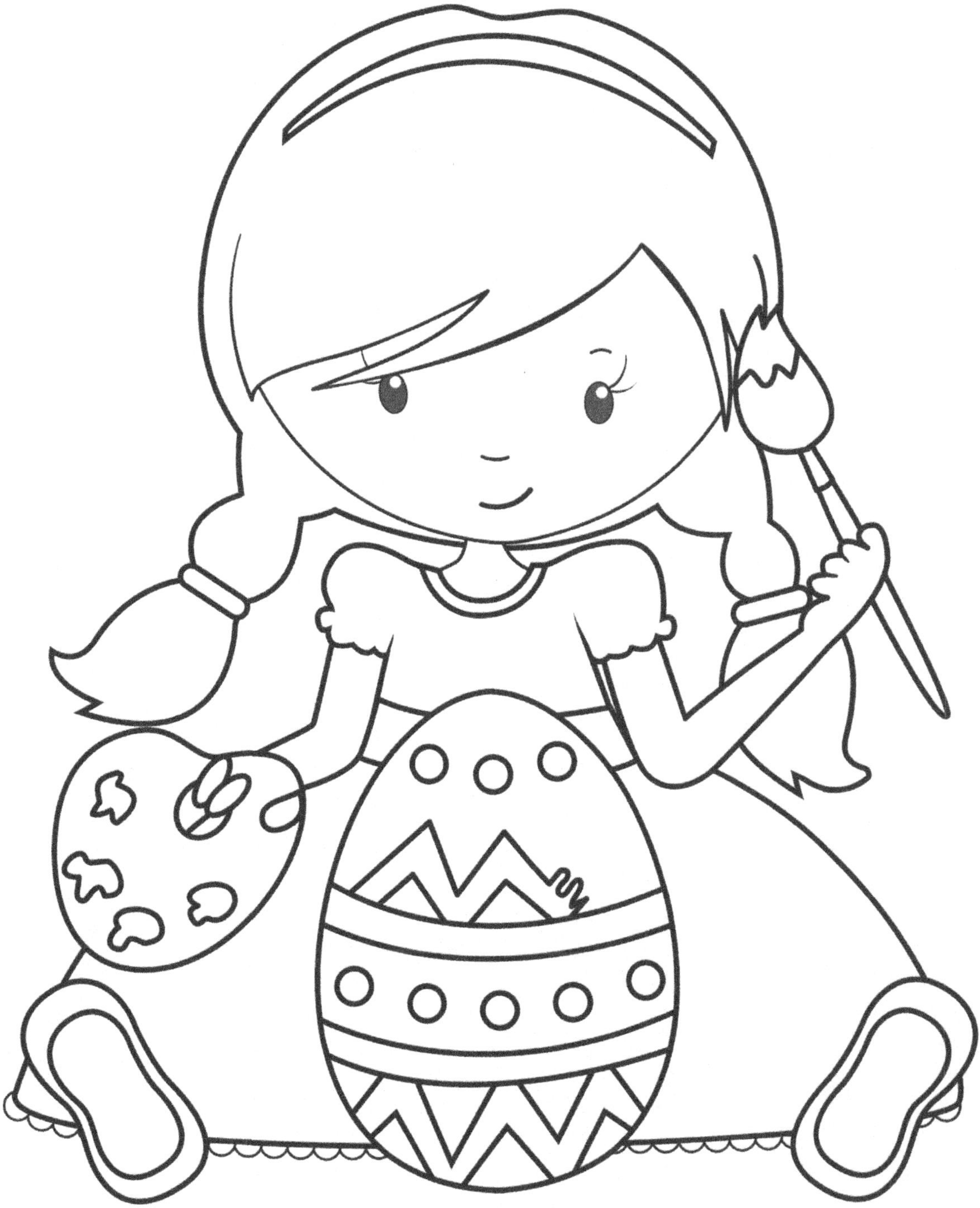

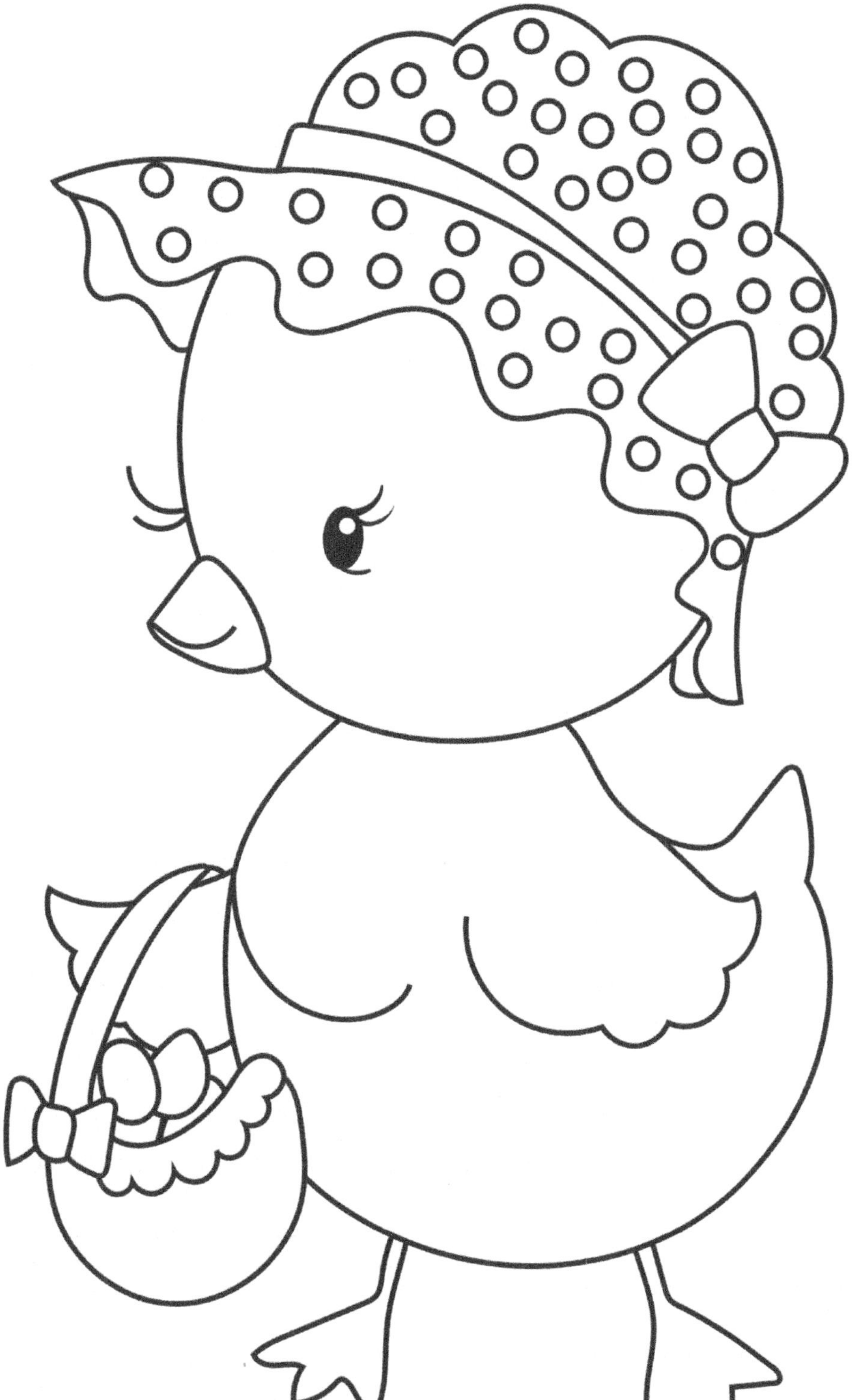

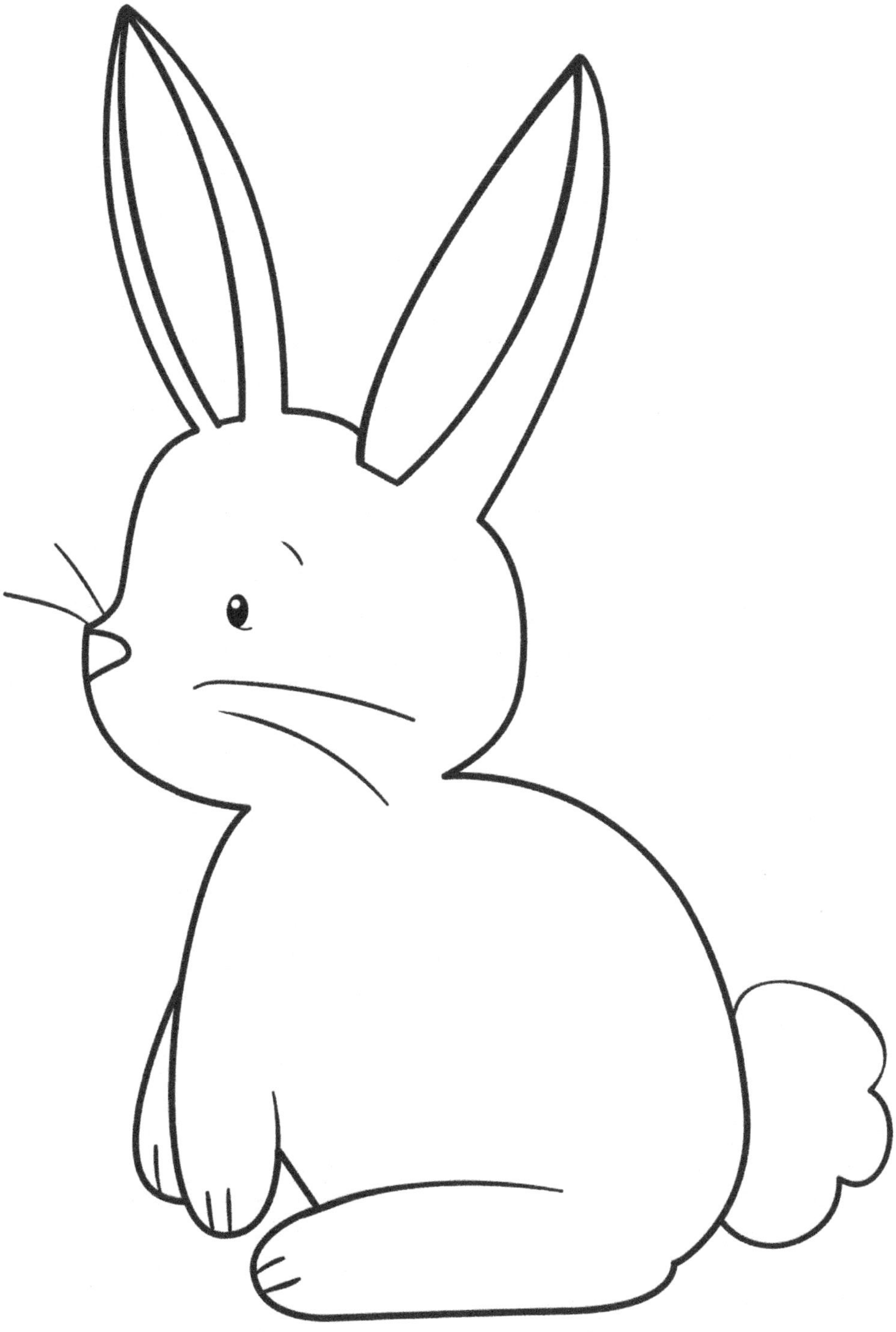

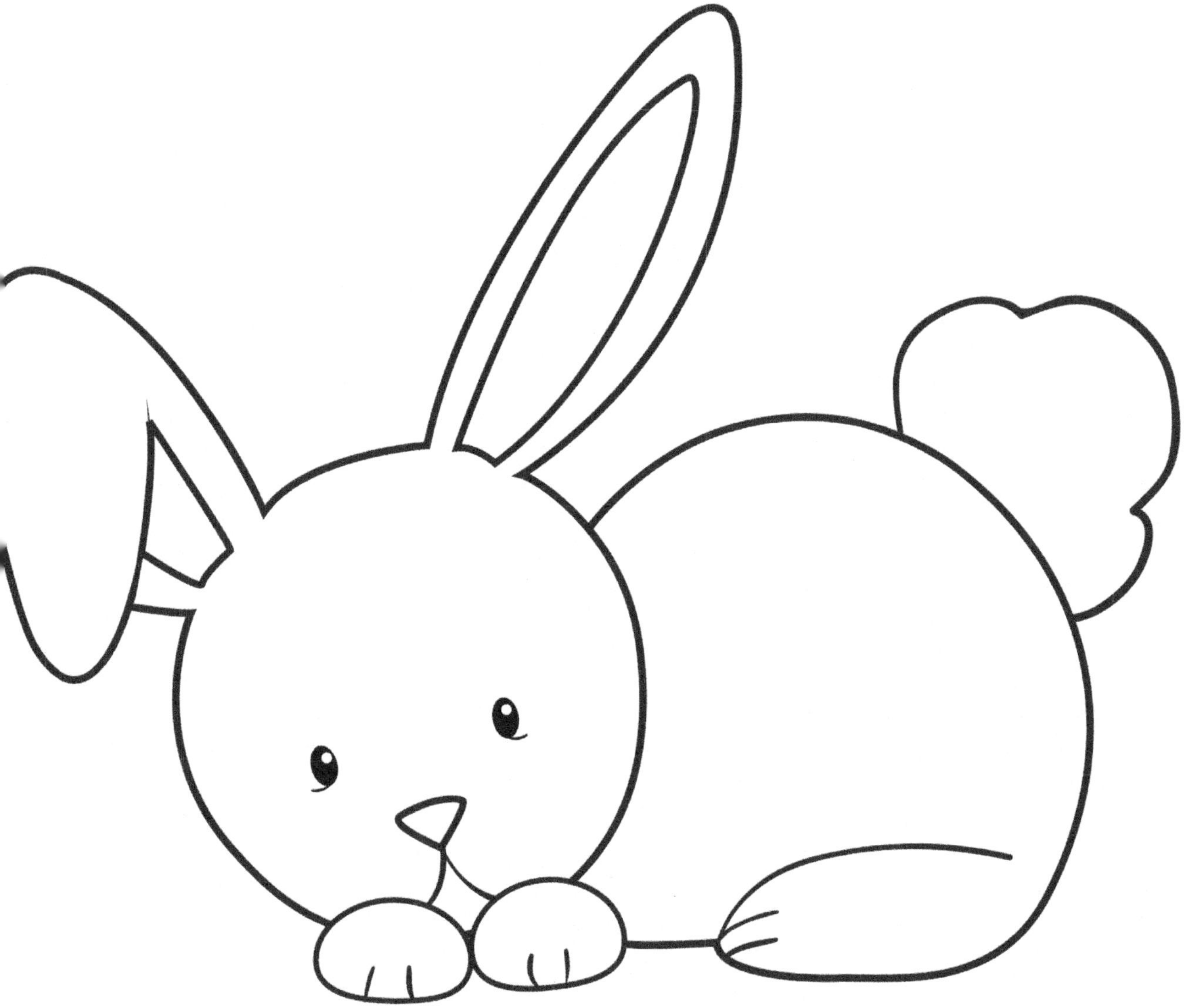

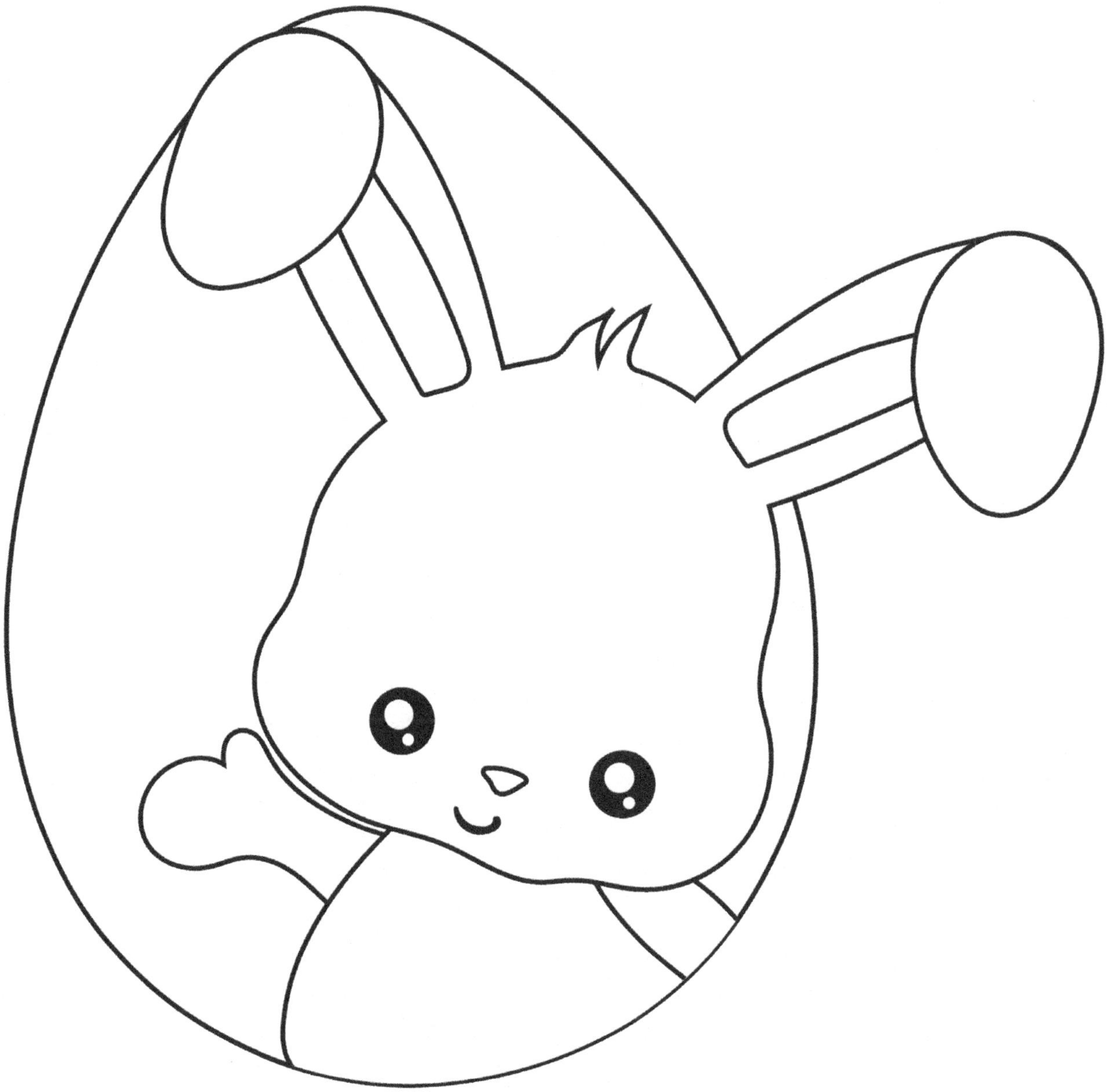

You CRACK me up

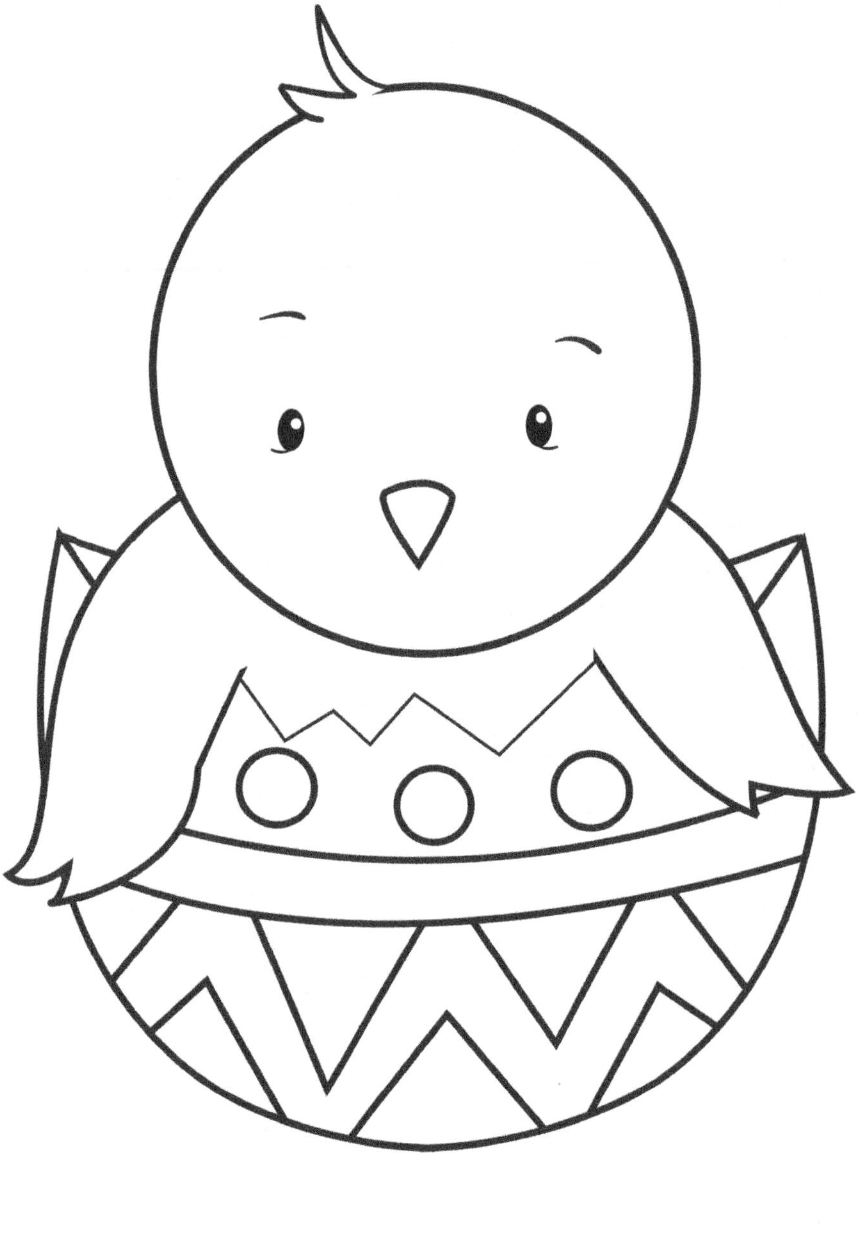

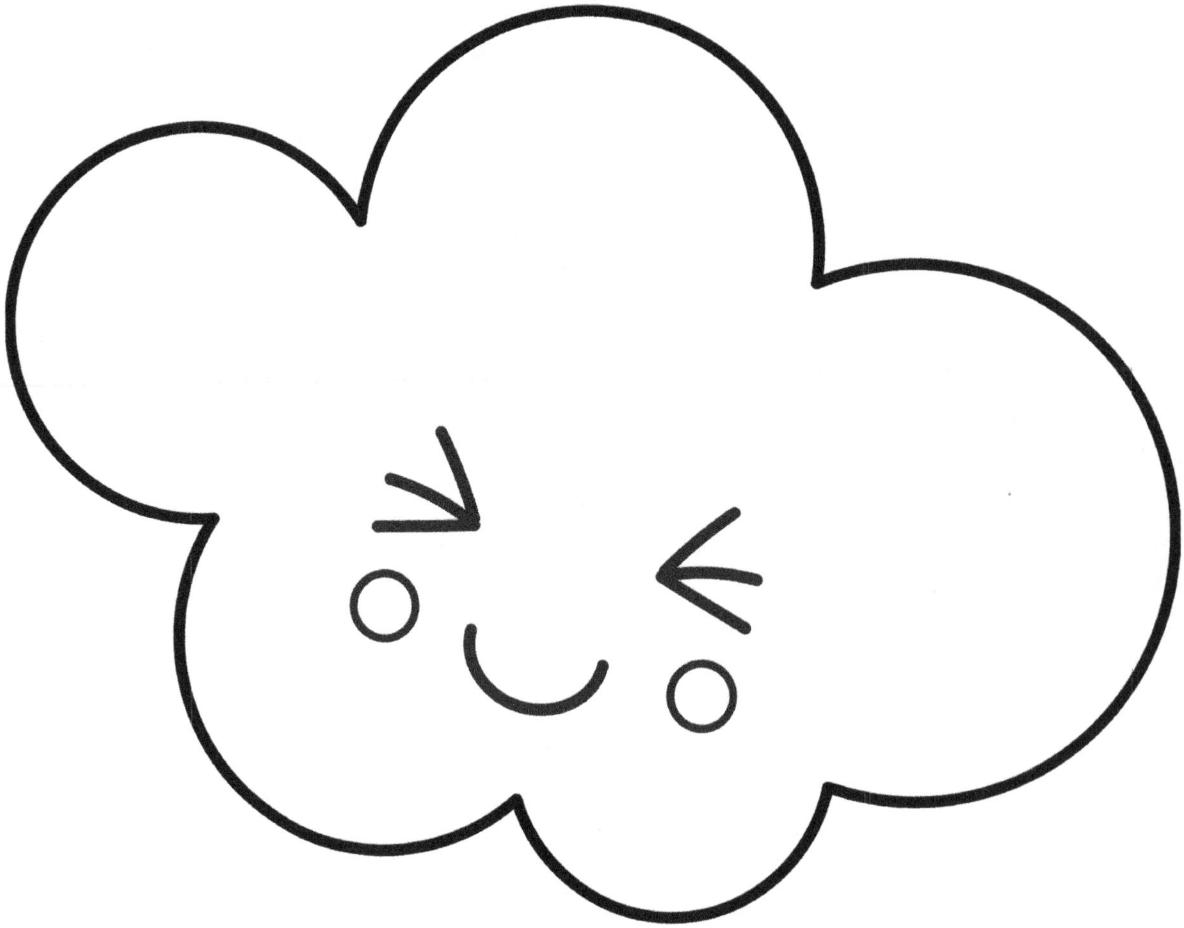

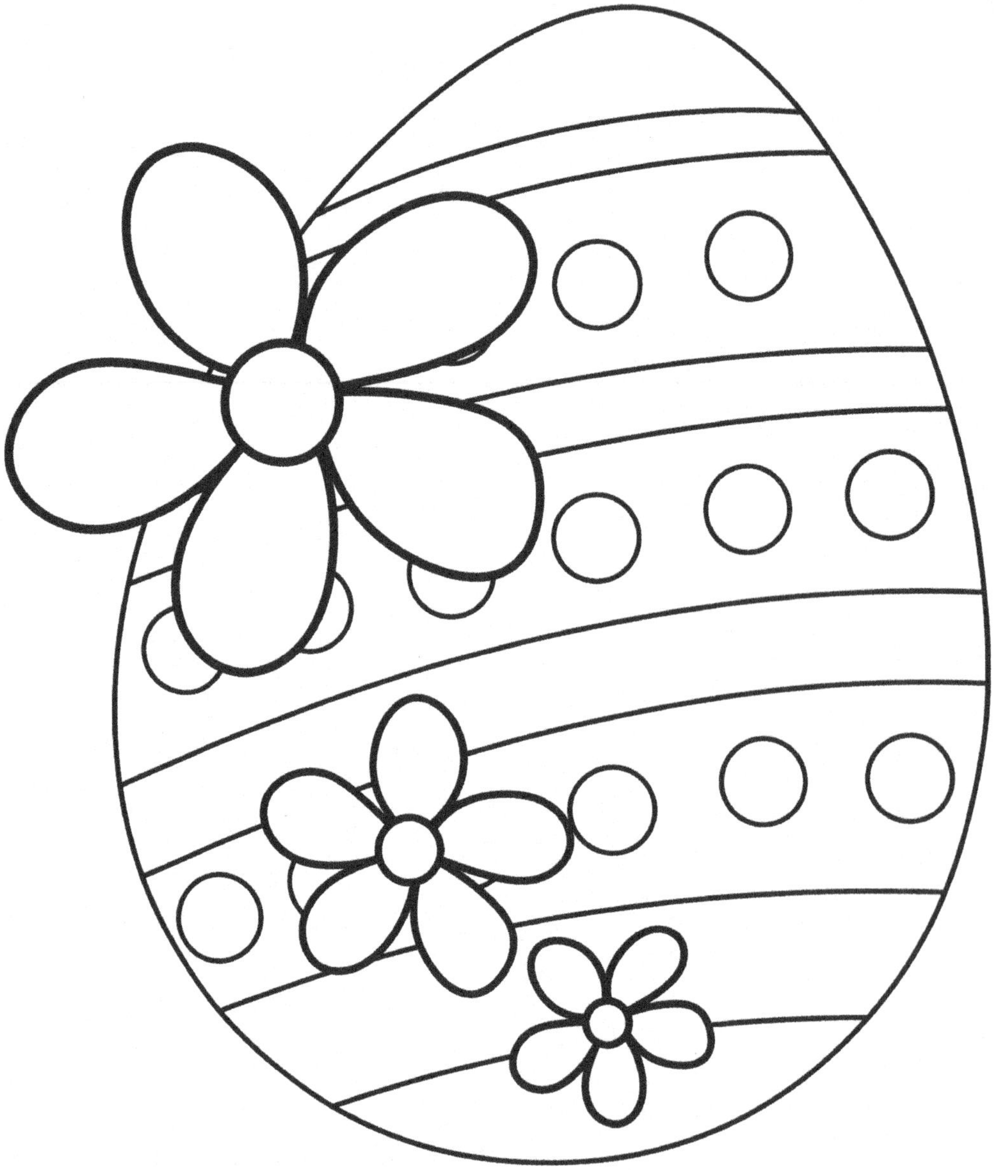

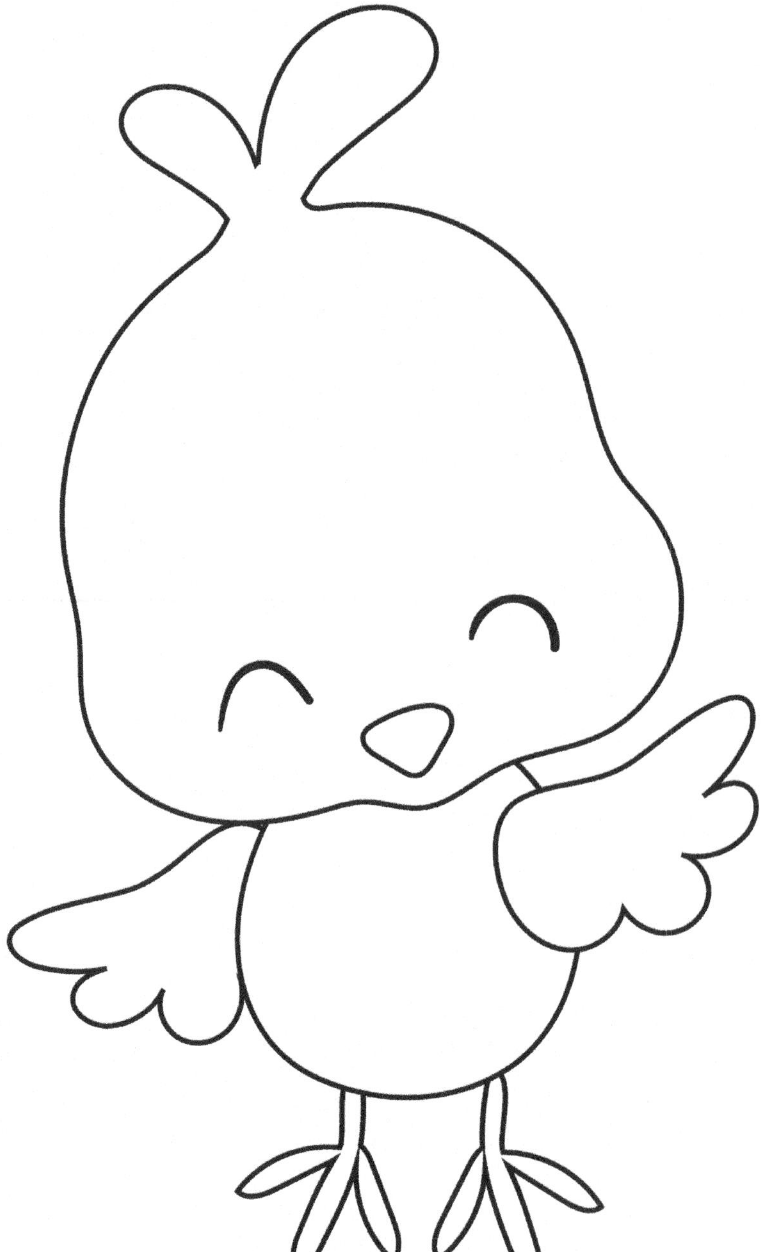

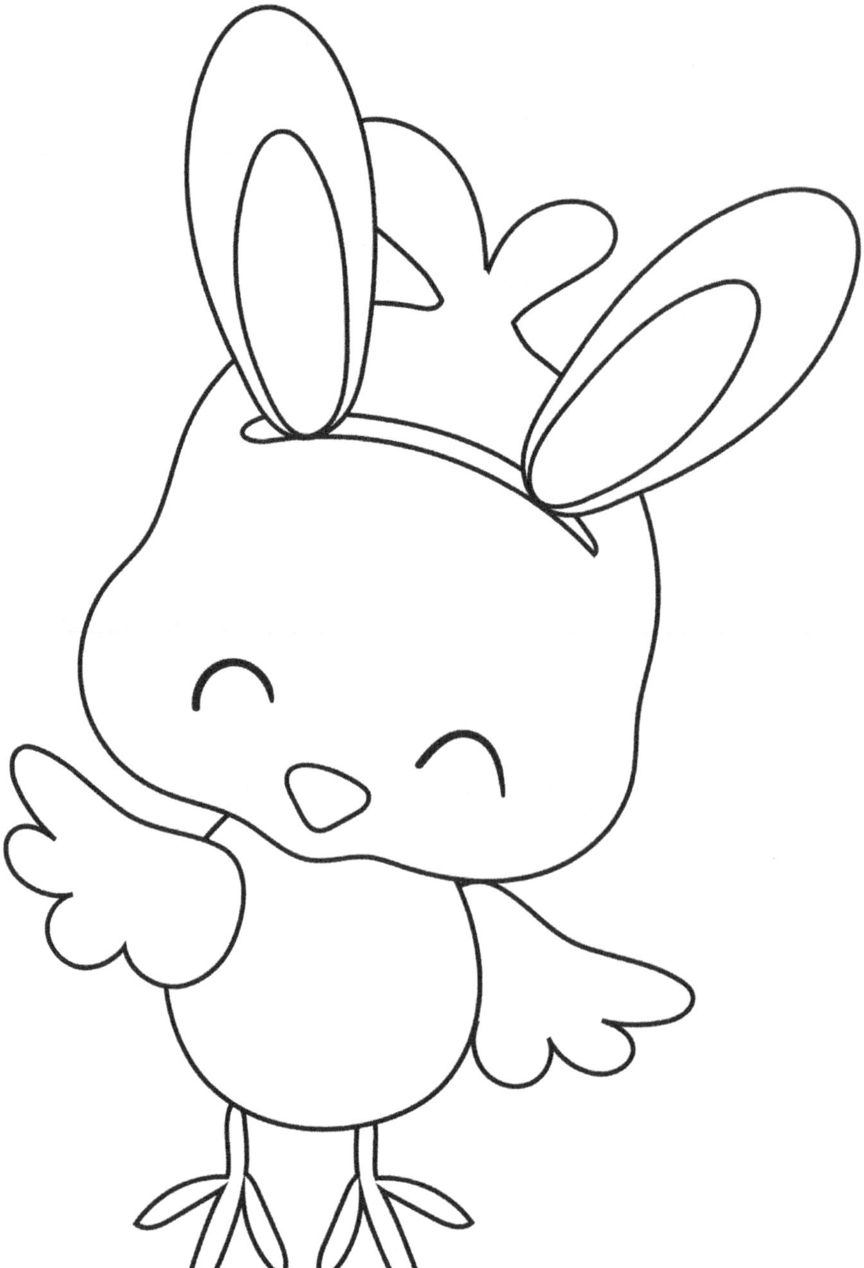

Hoppy Easter

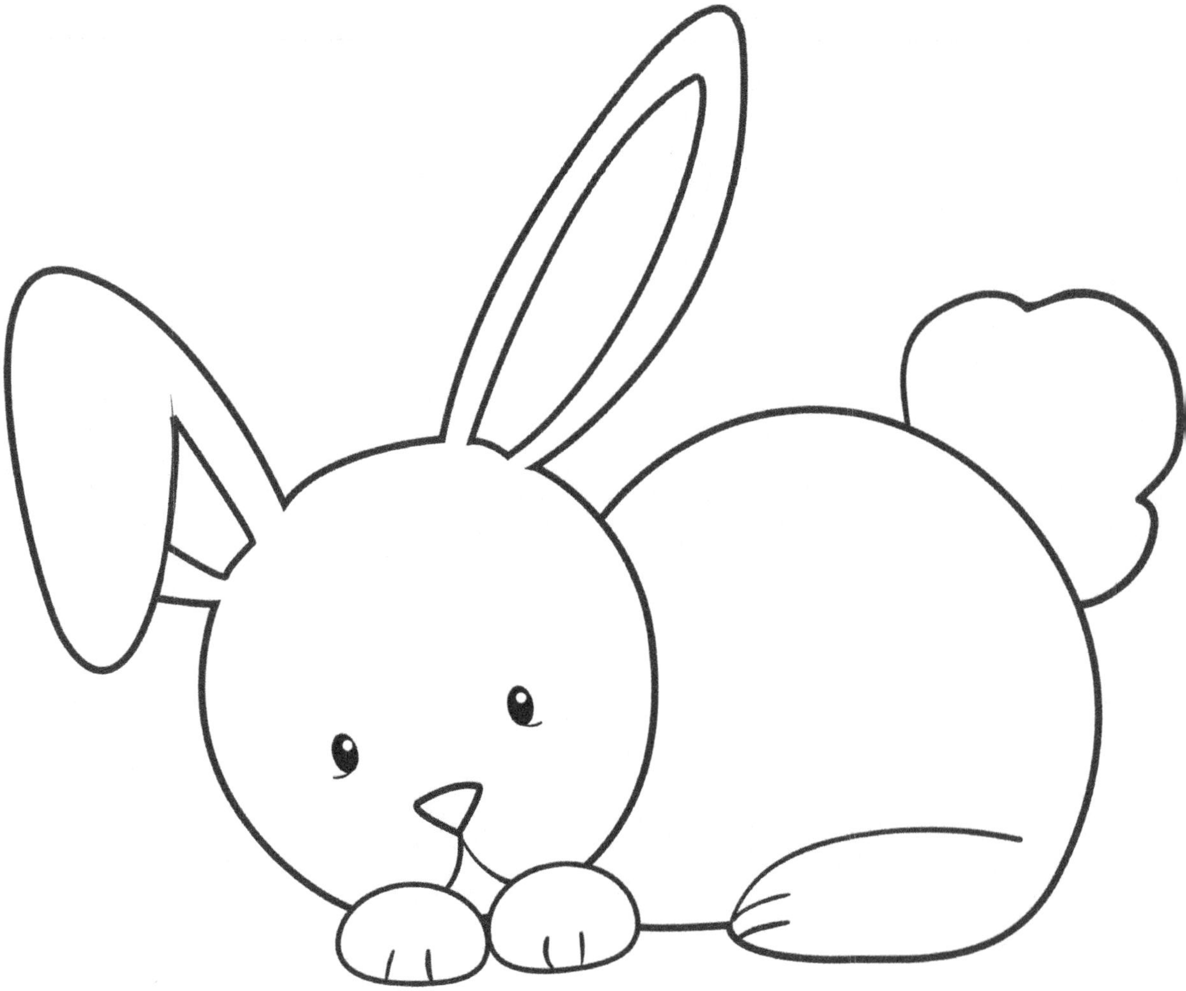

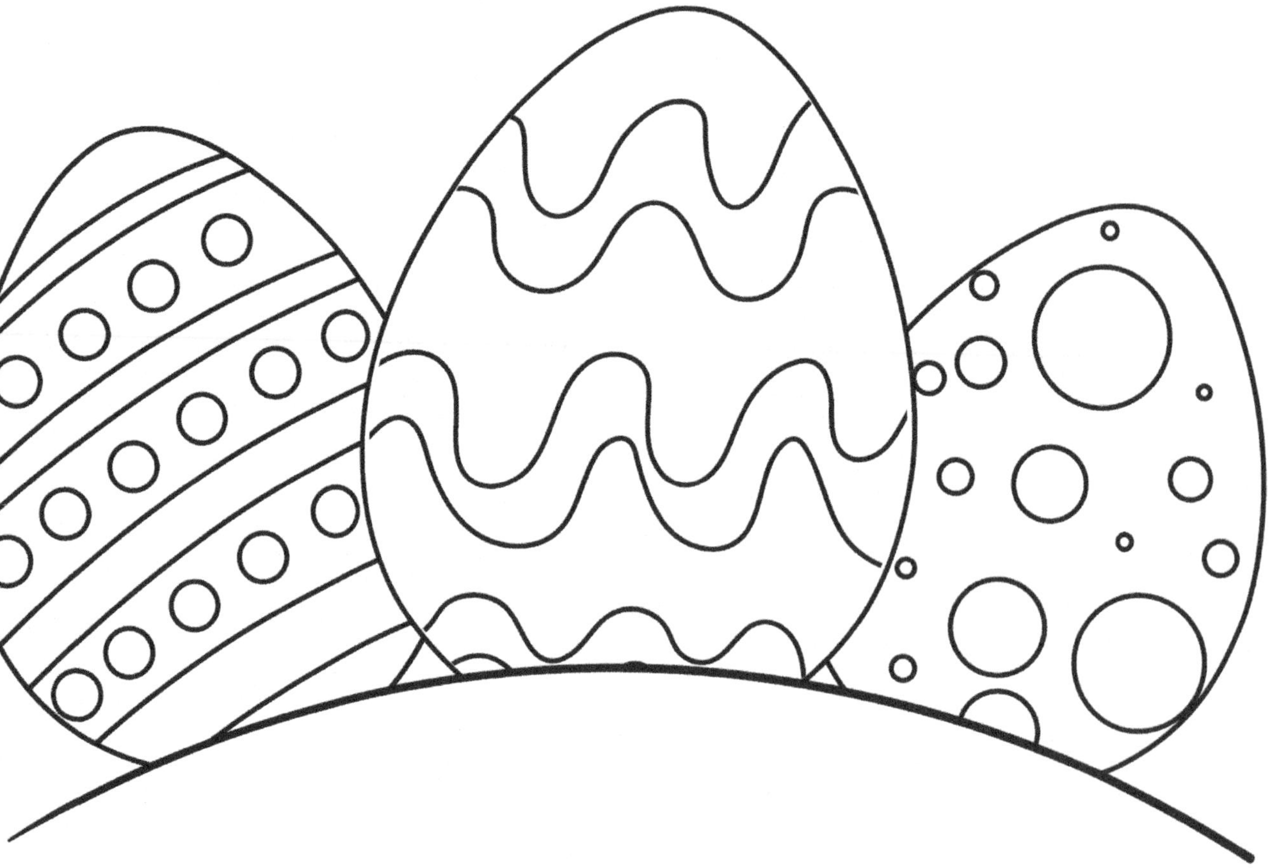

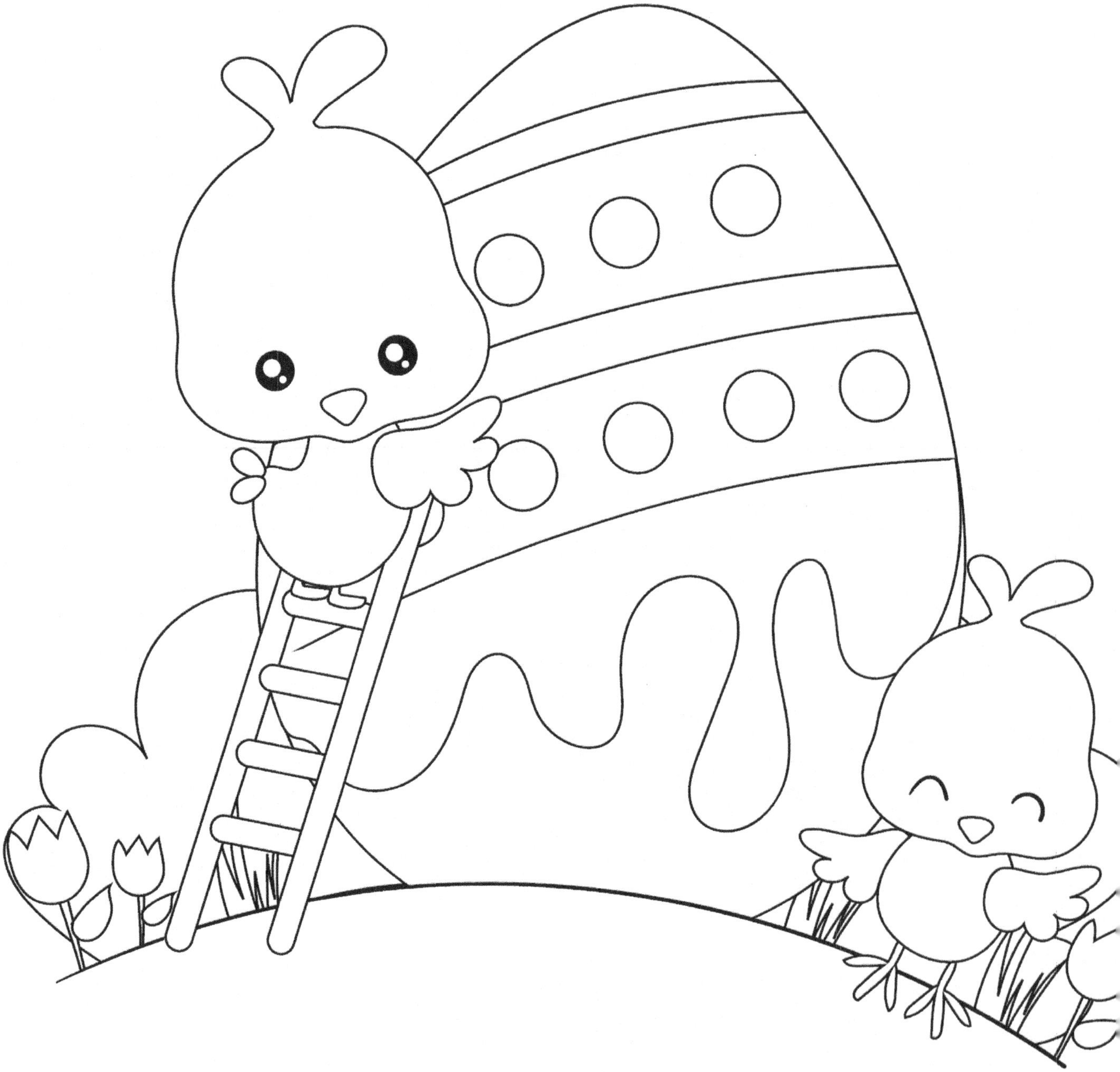

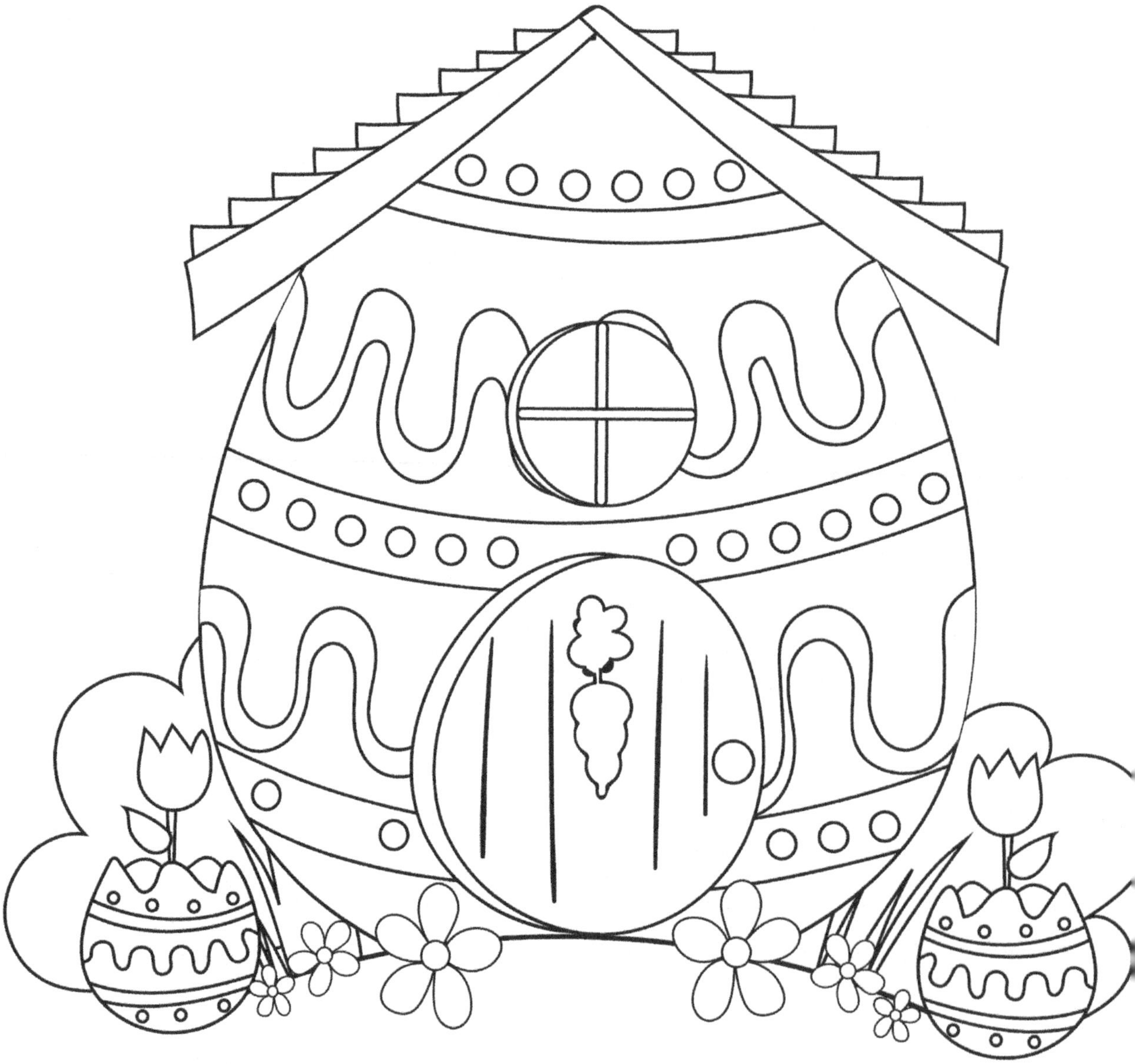

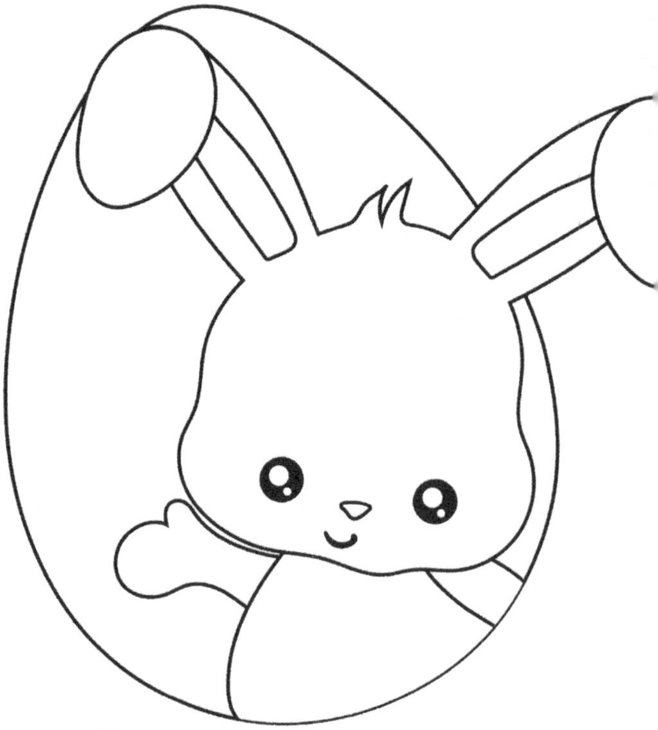

Some Bunny Loves You

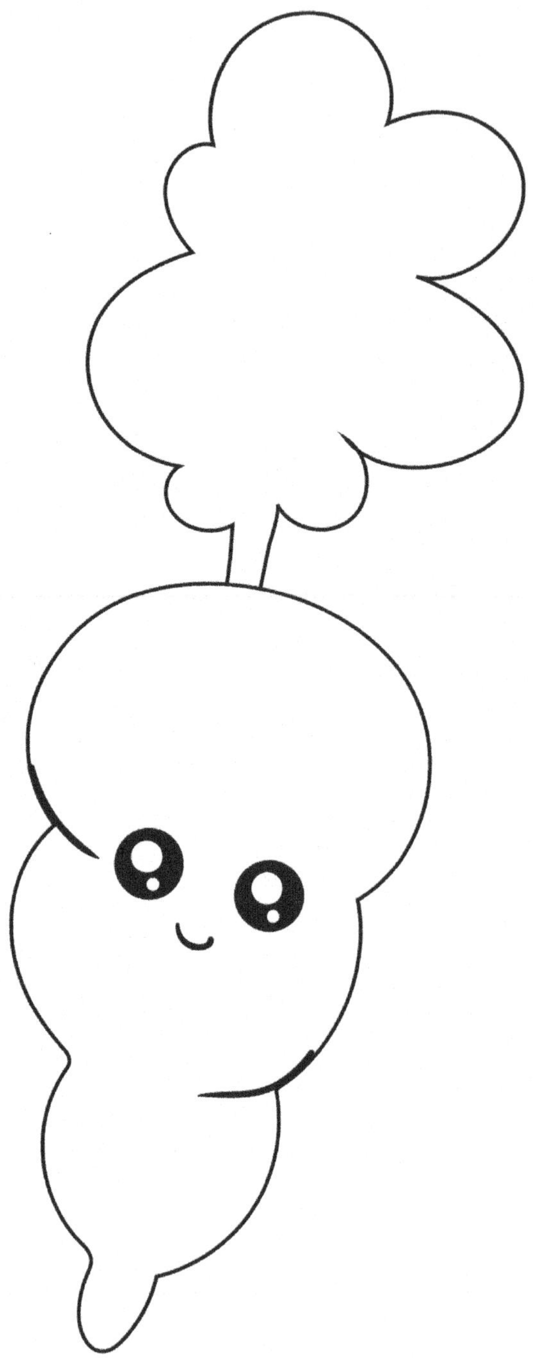

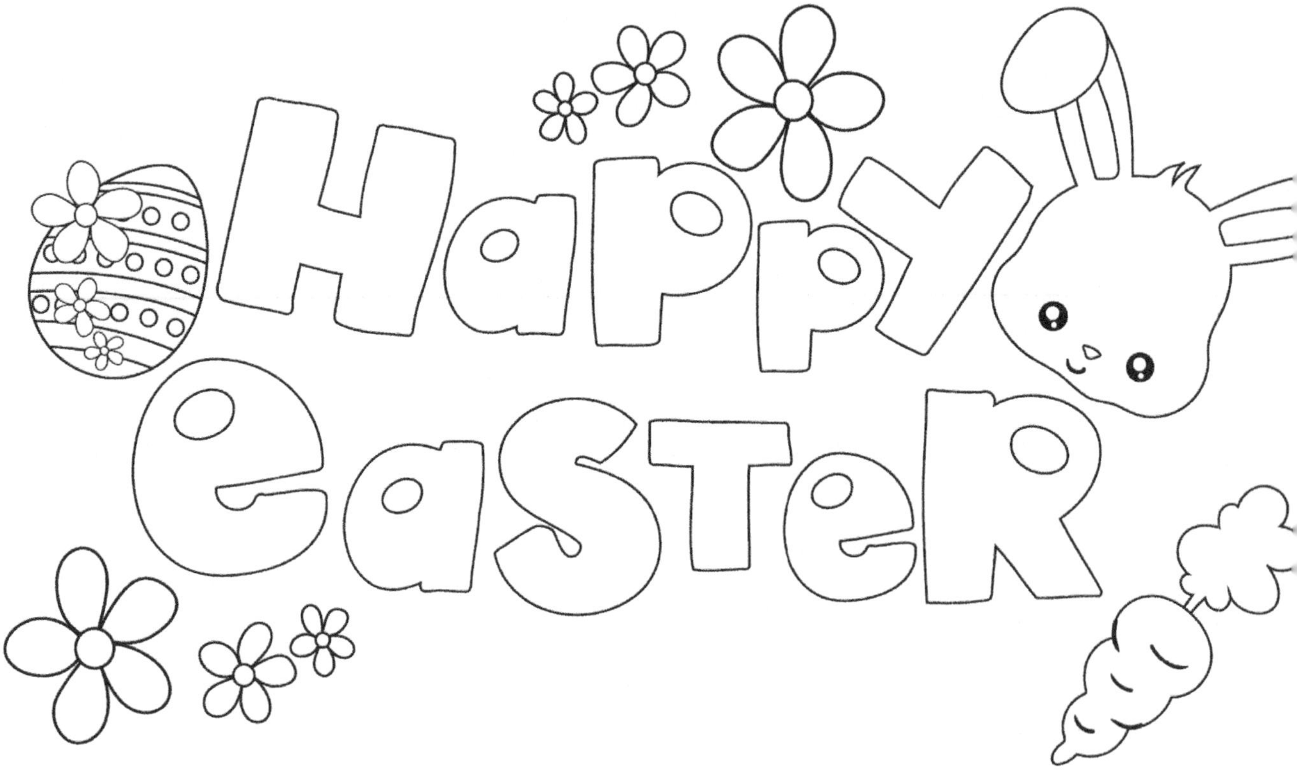
Happy
Easter

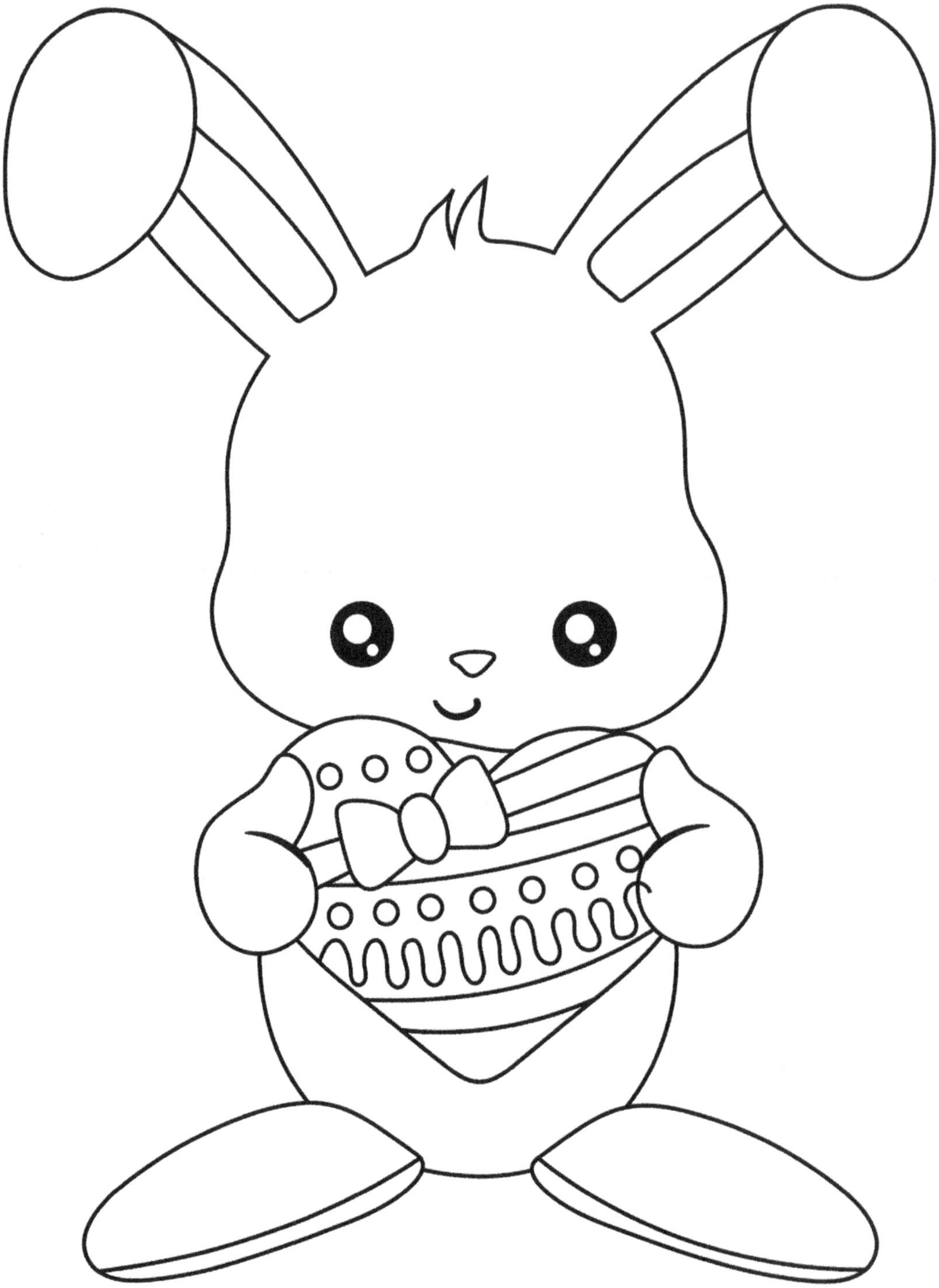

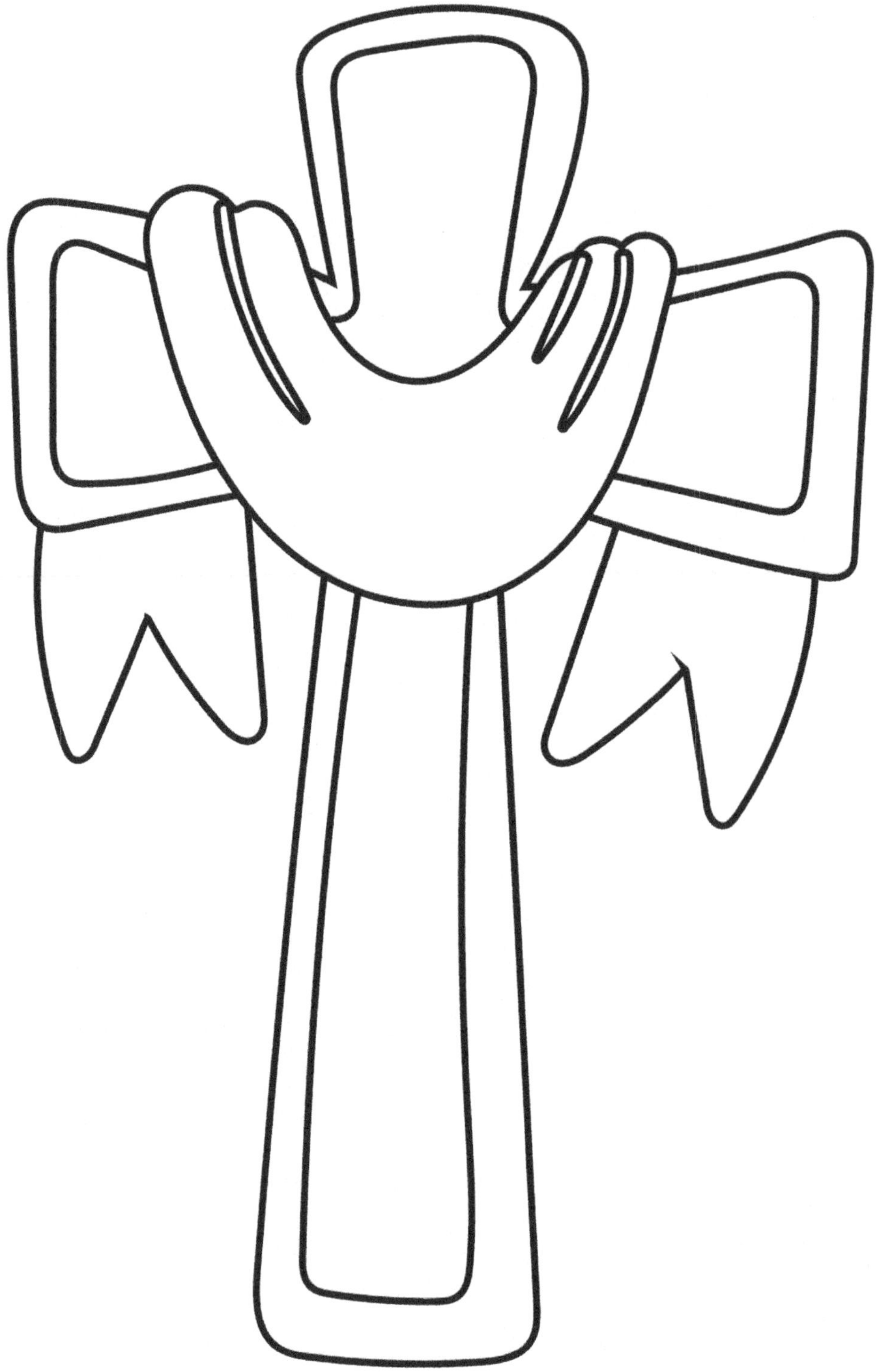

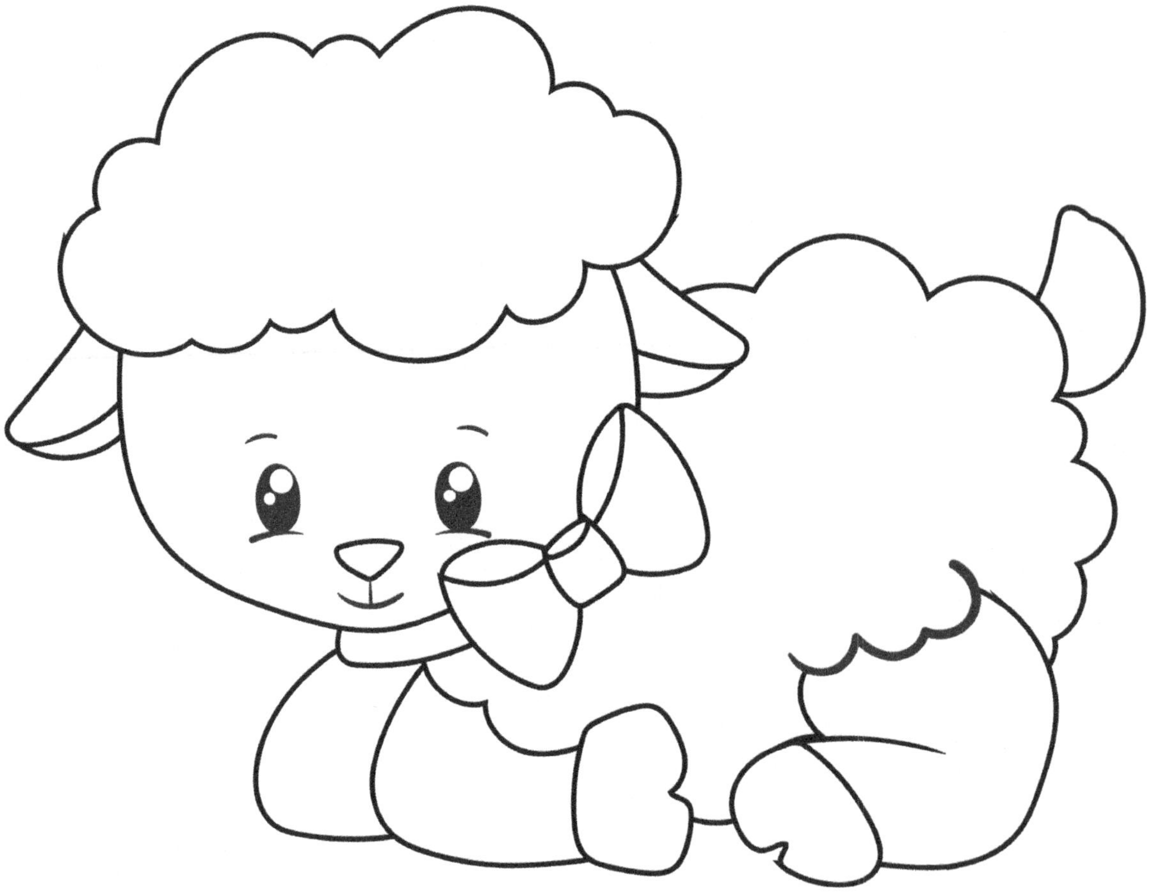

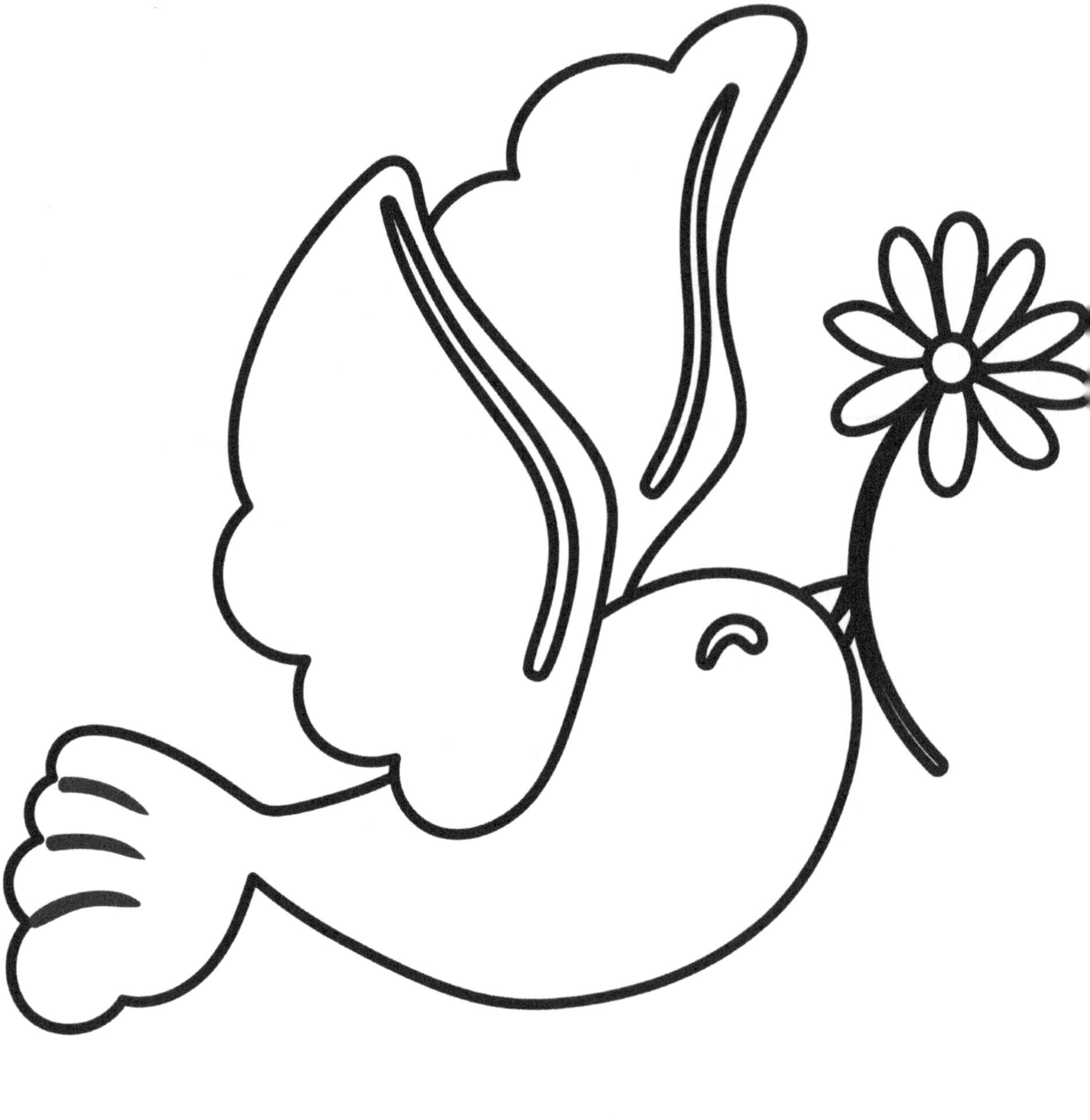

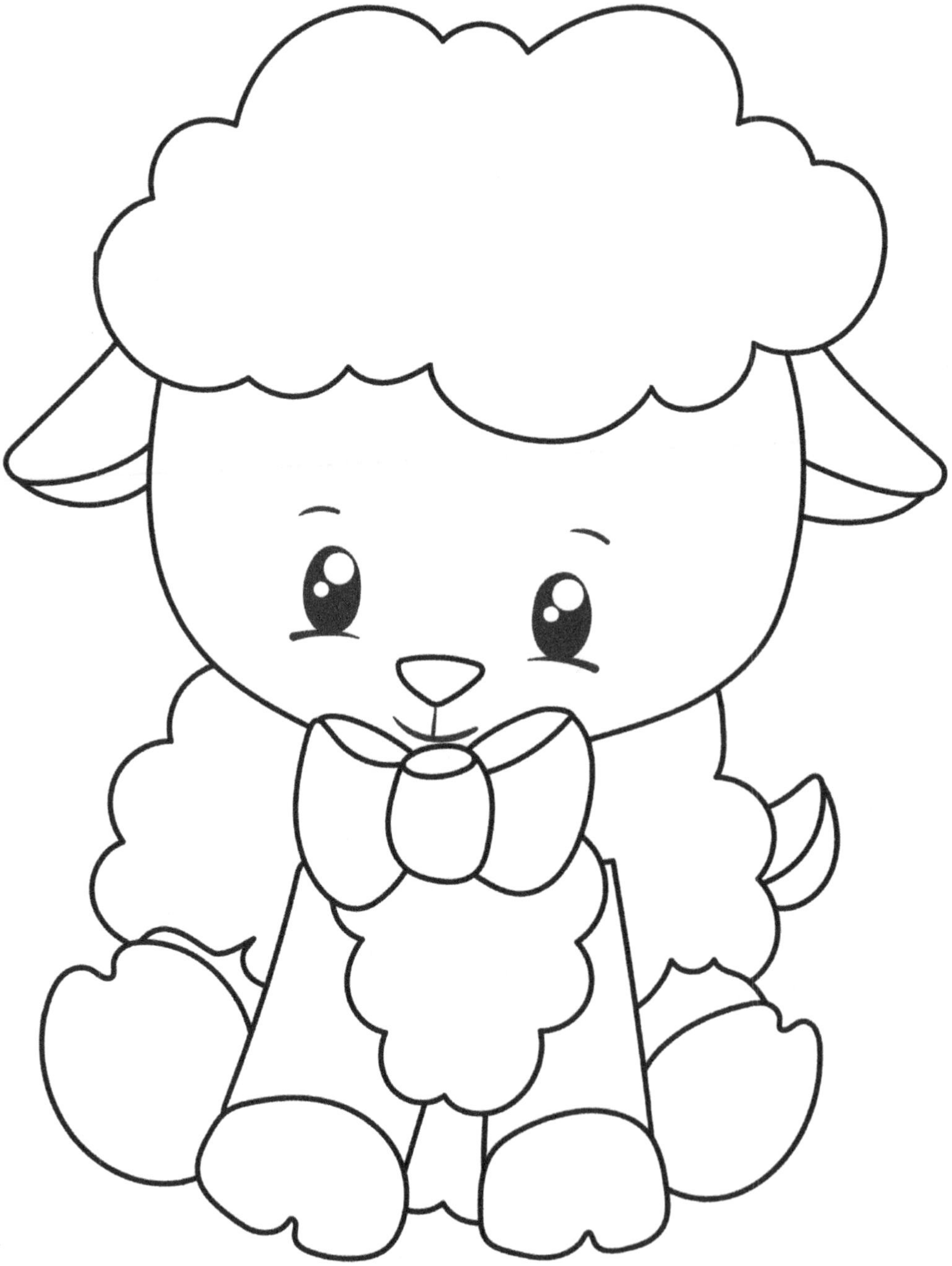

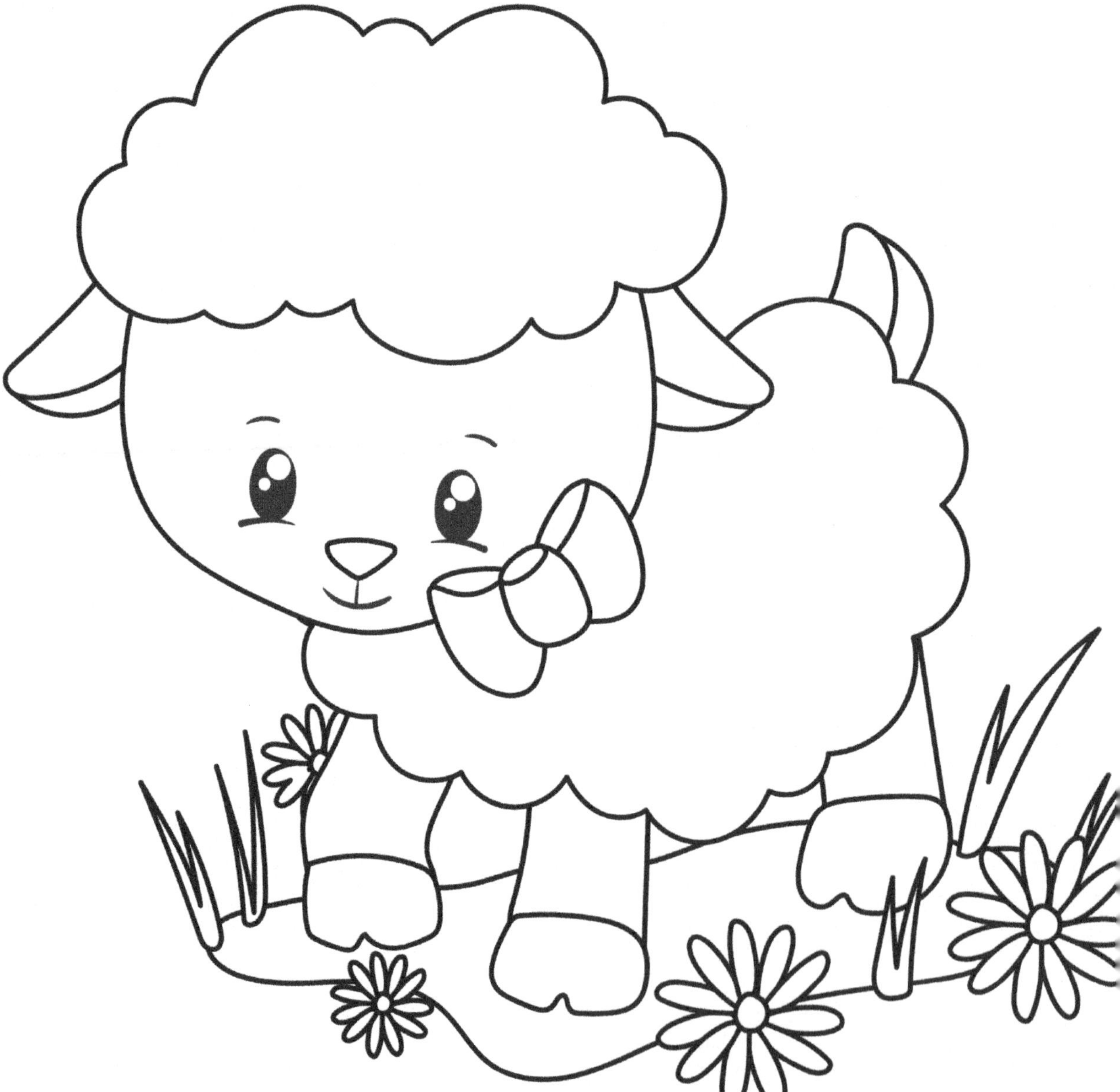

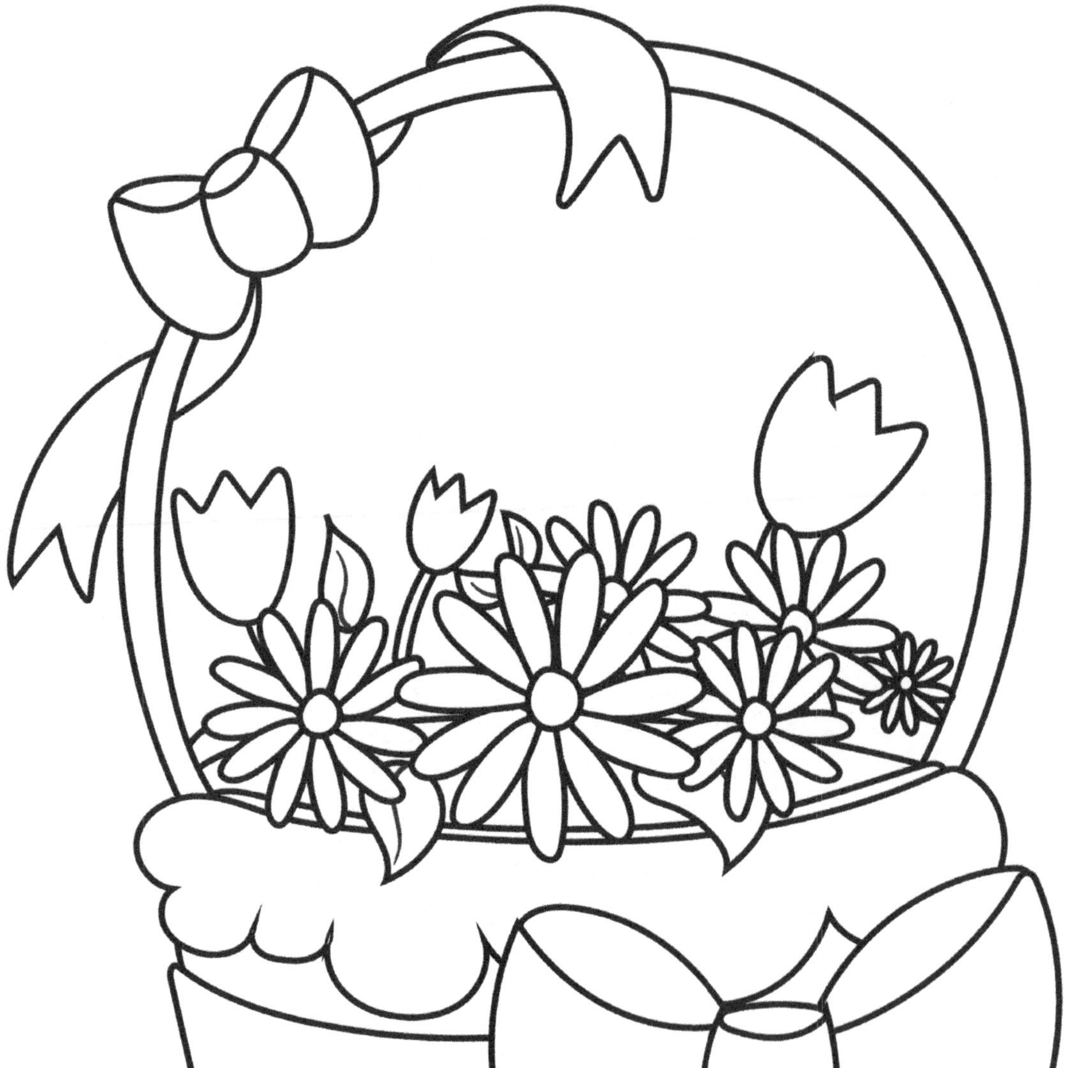

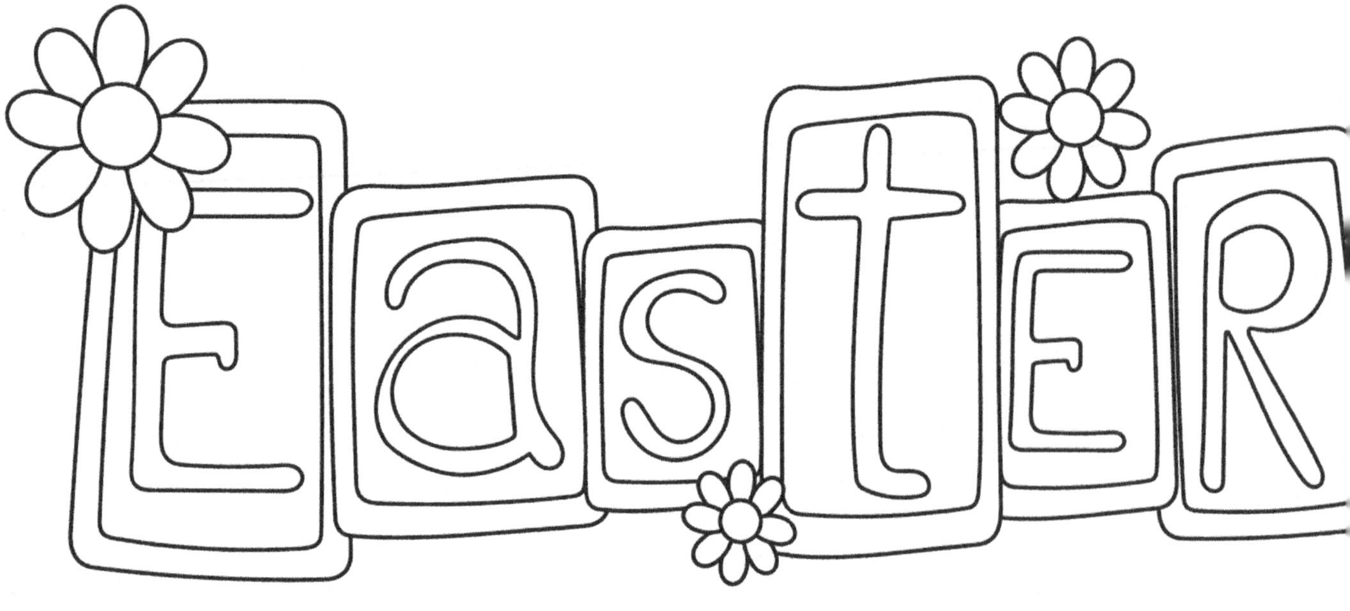
Easter

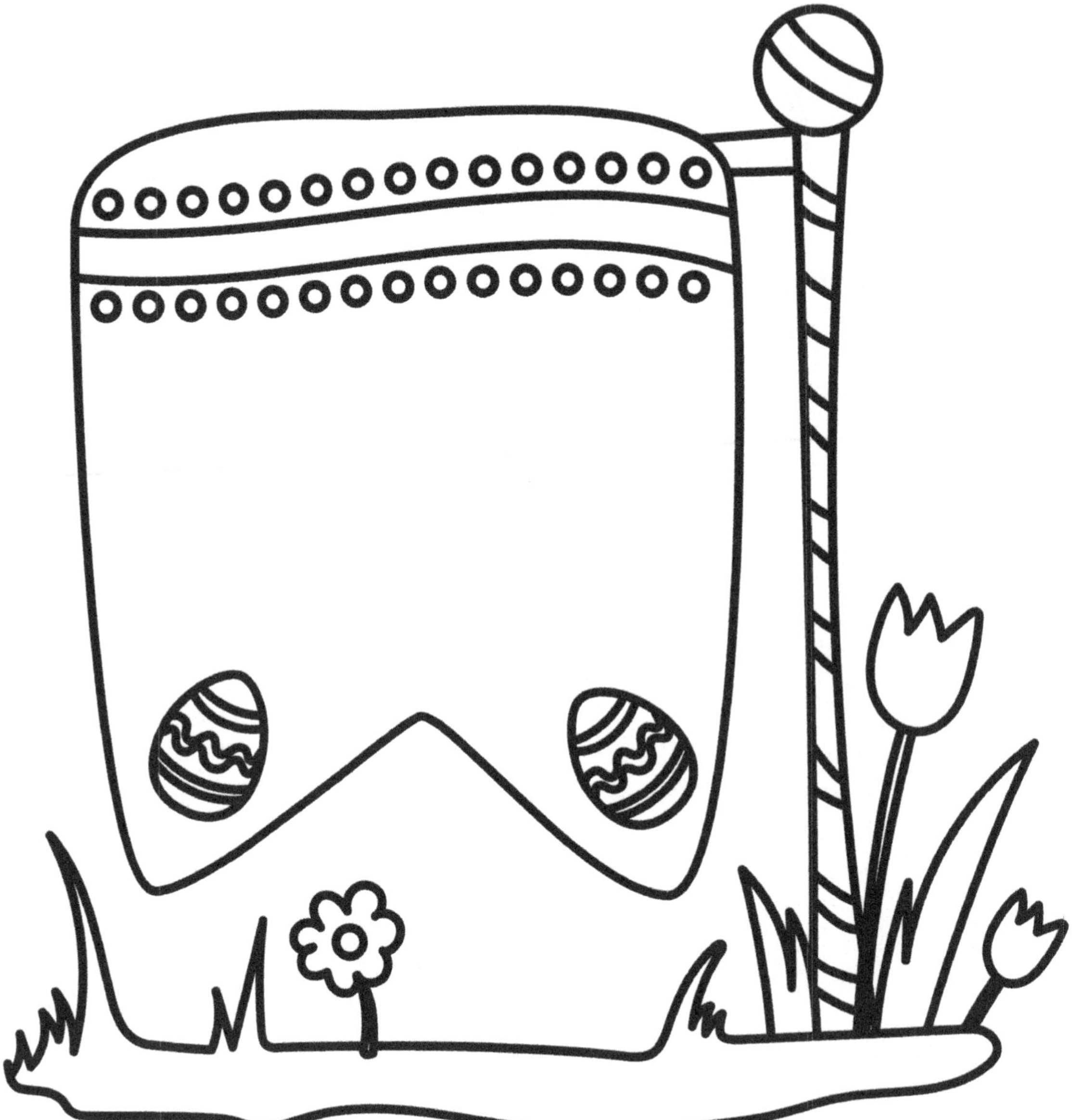

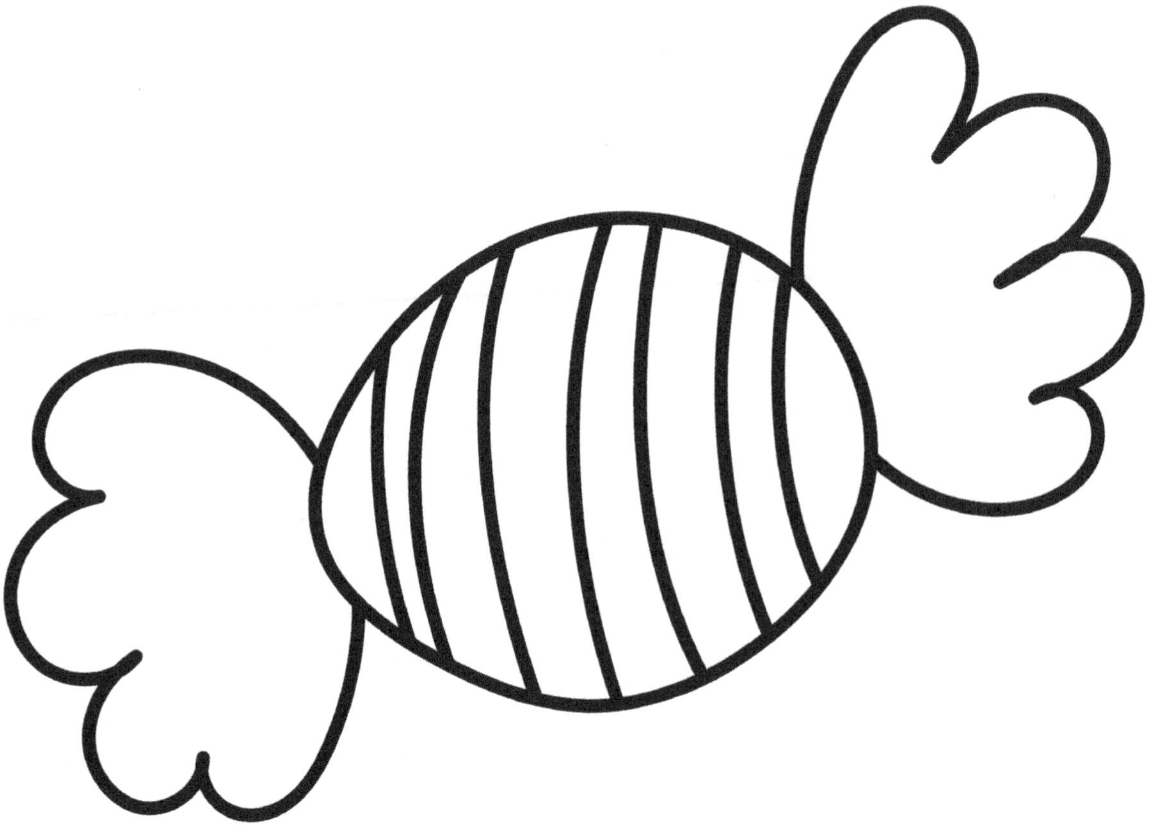

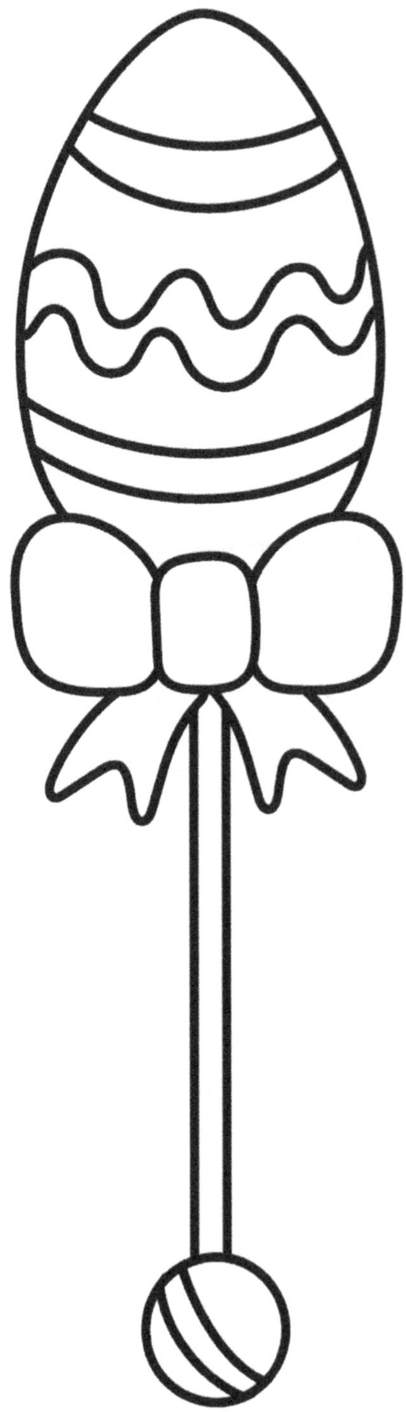

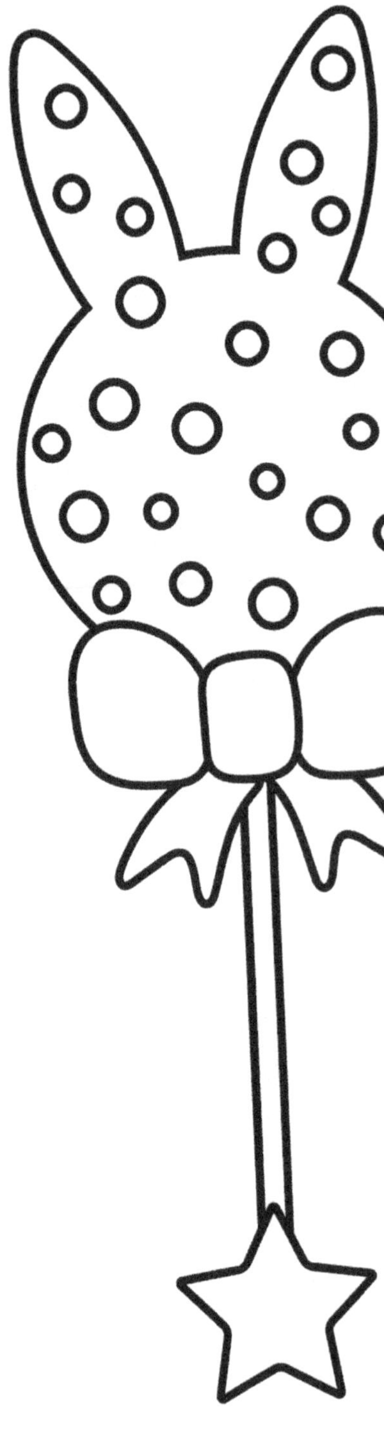

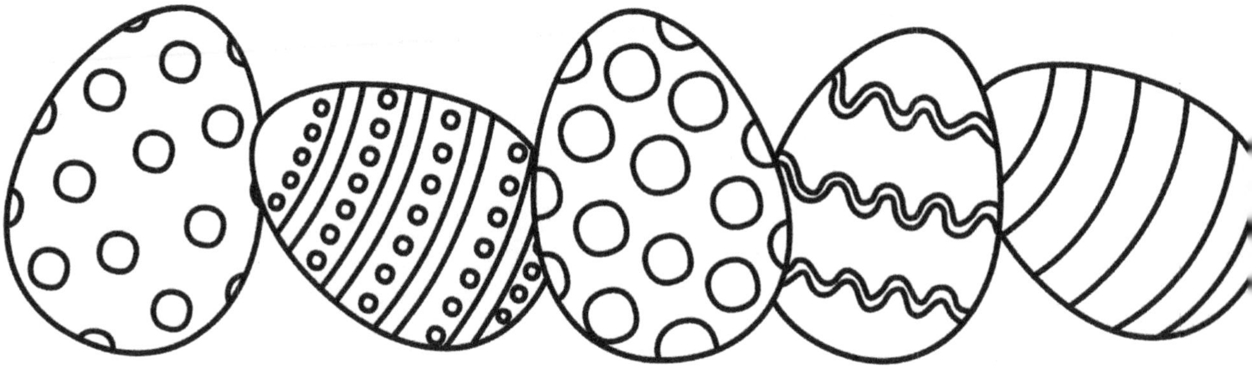

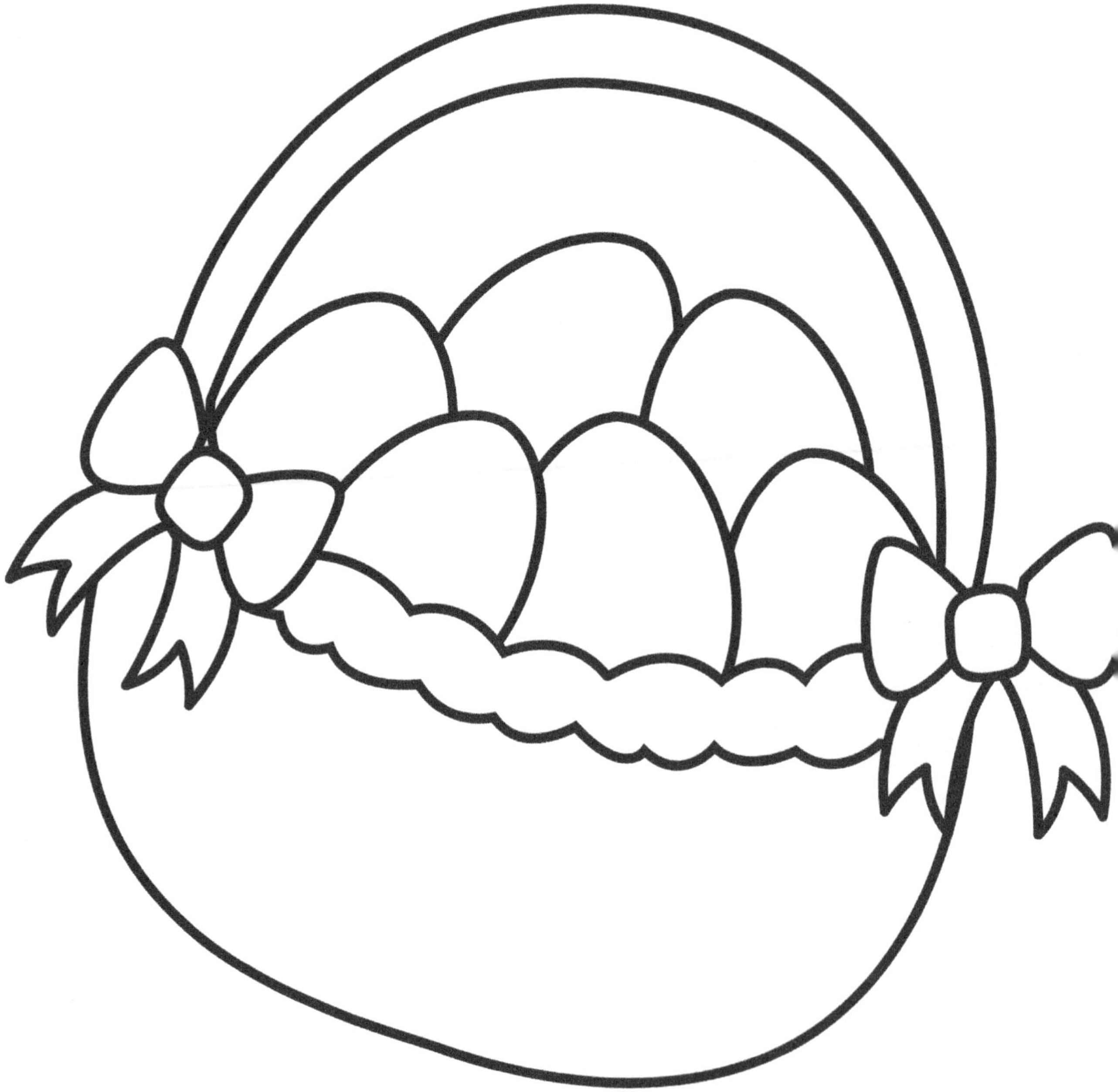

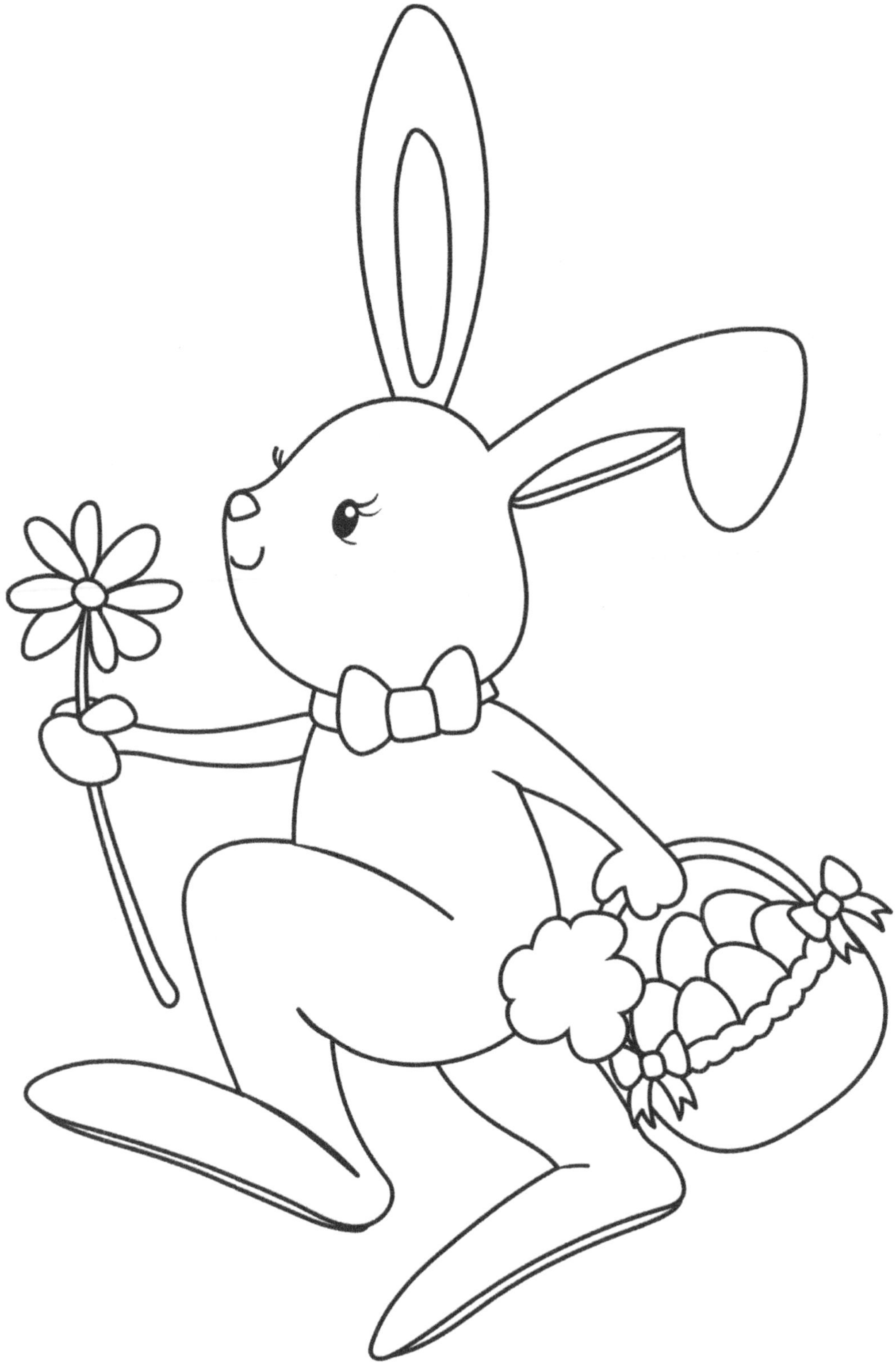

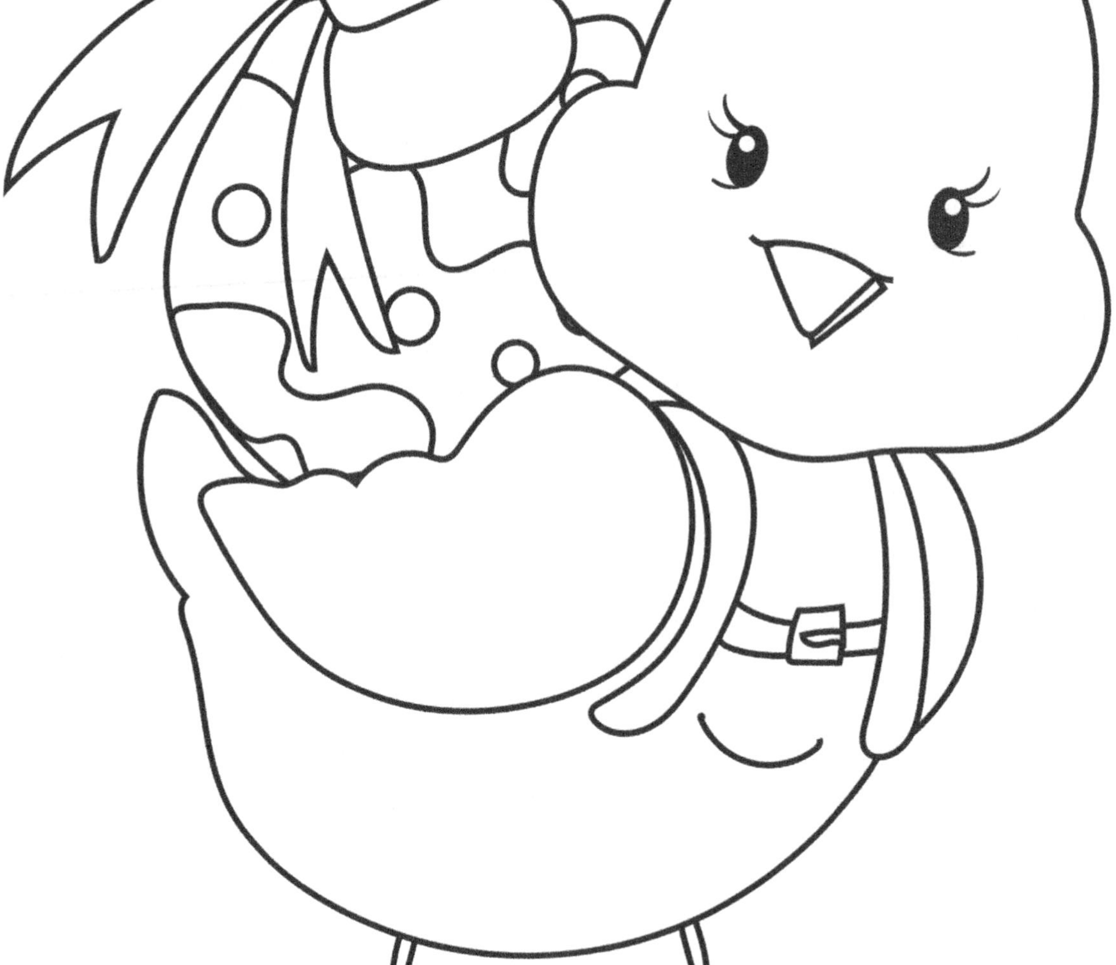

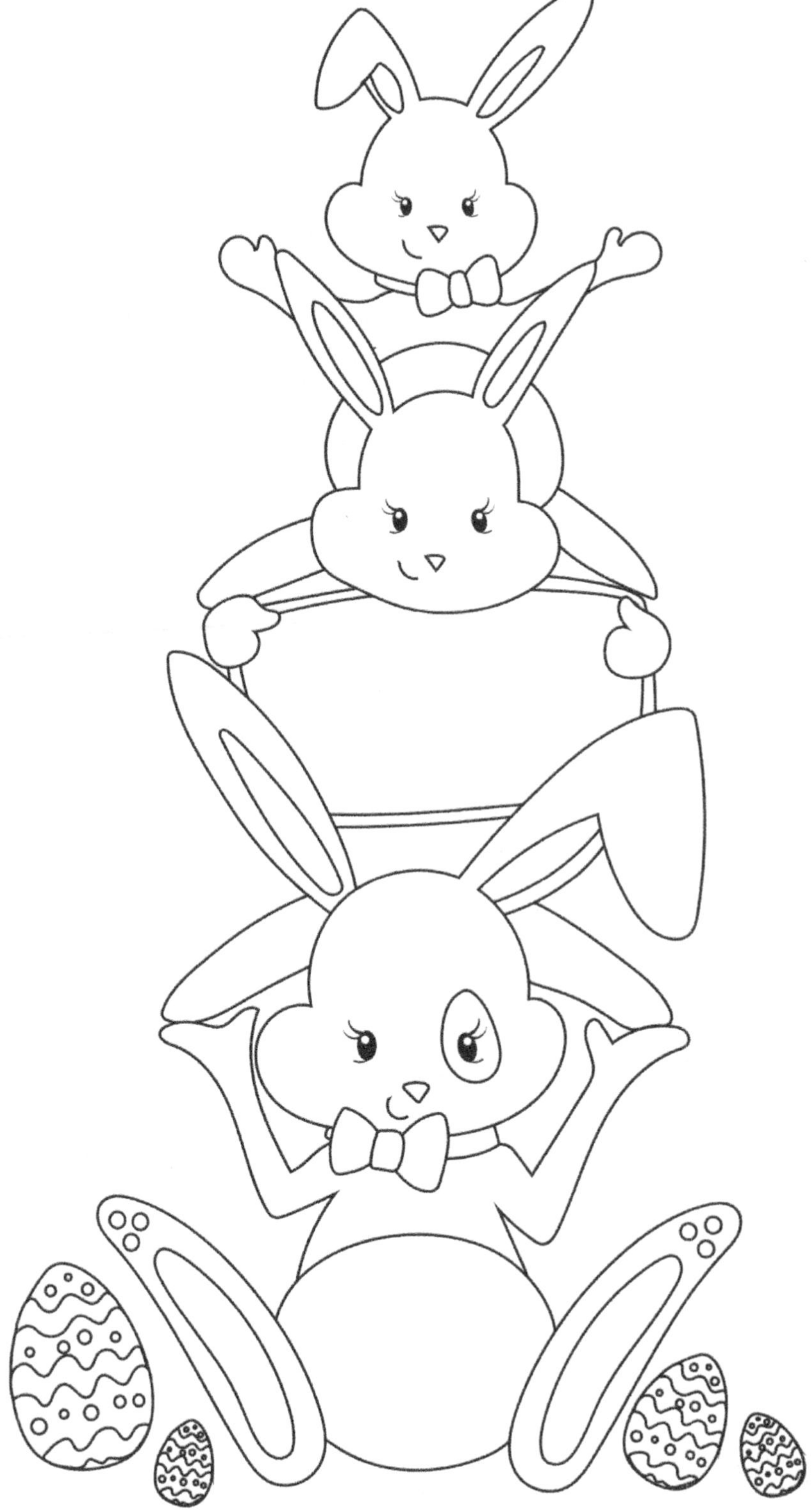

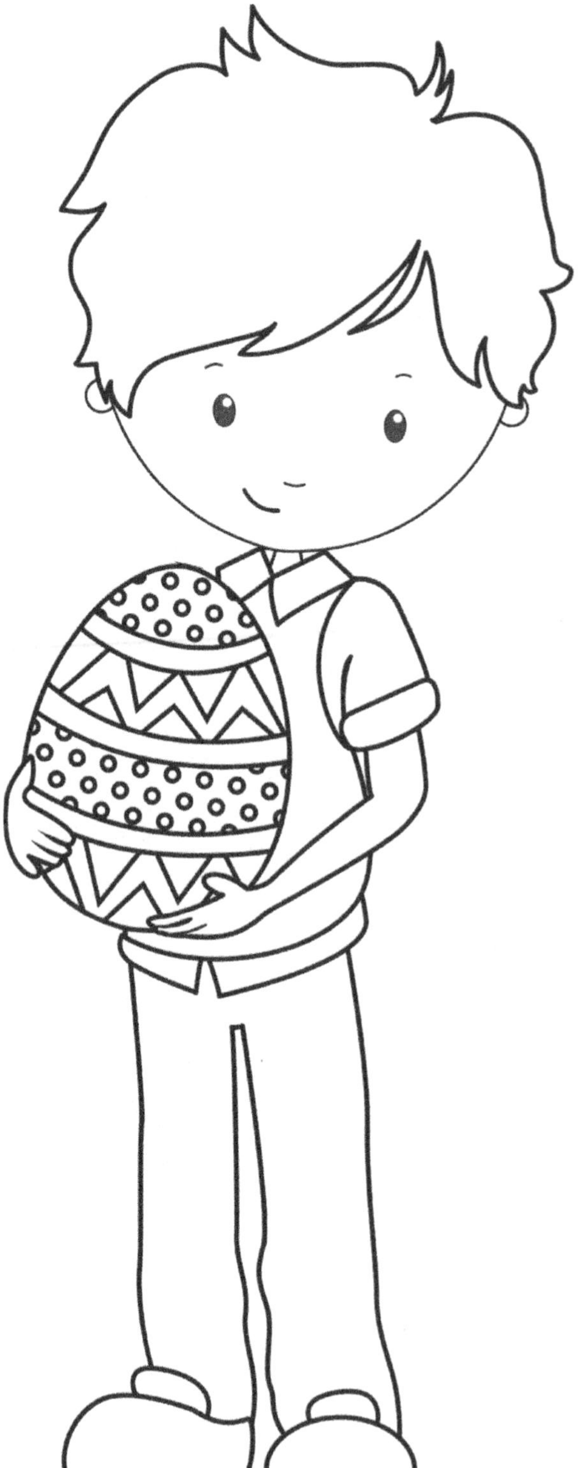

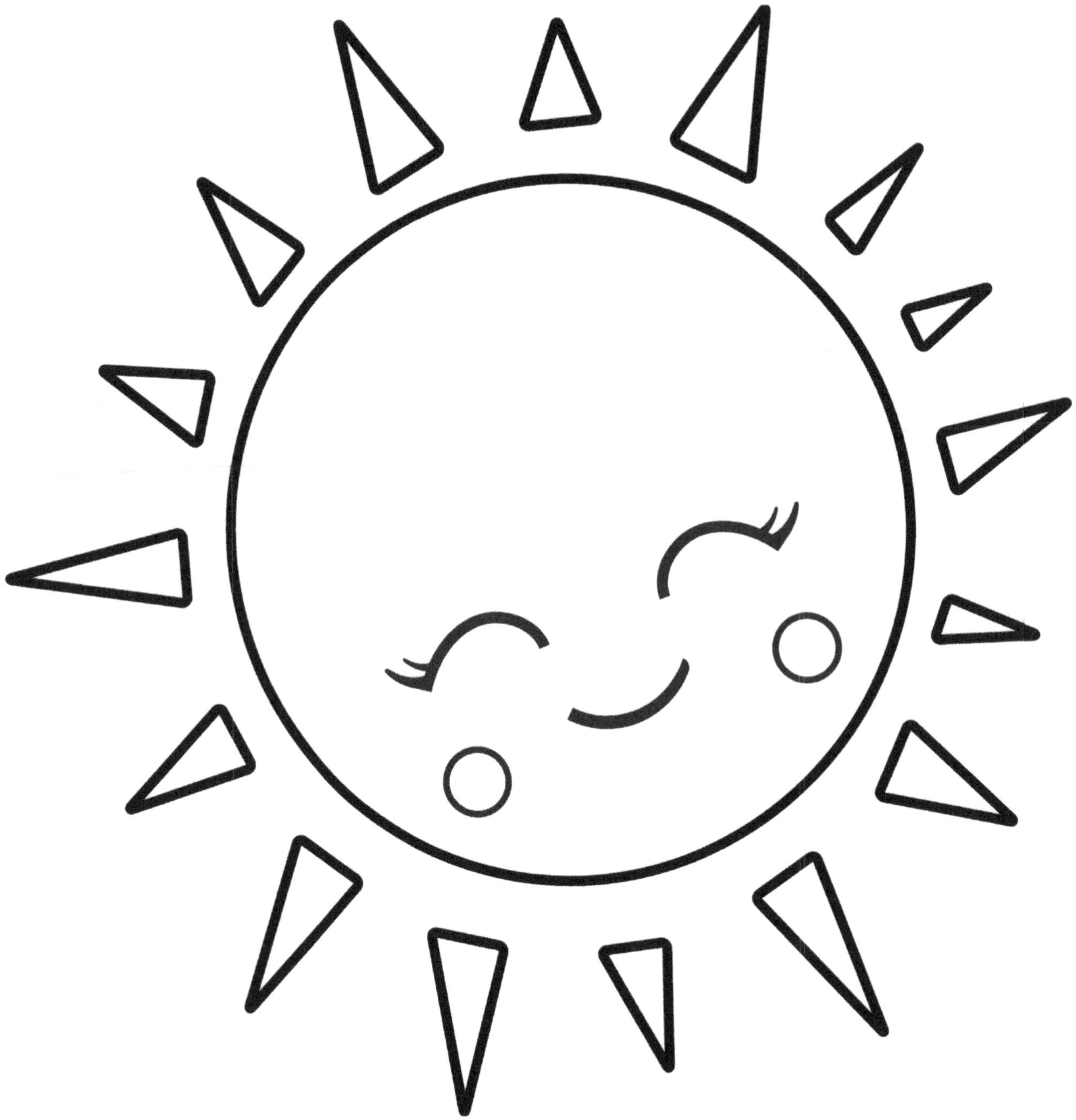

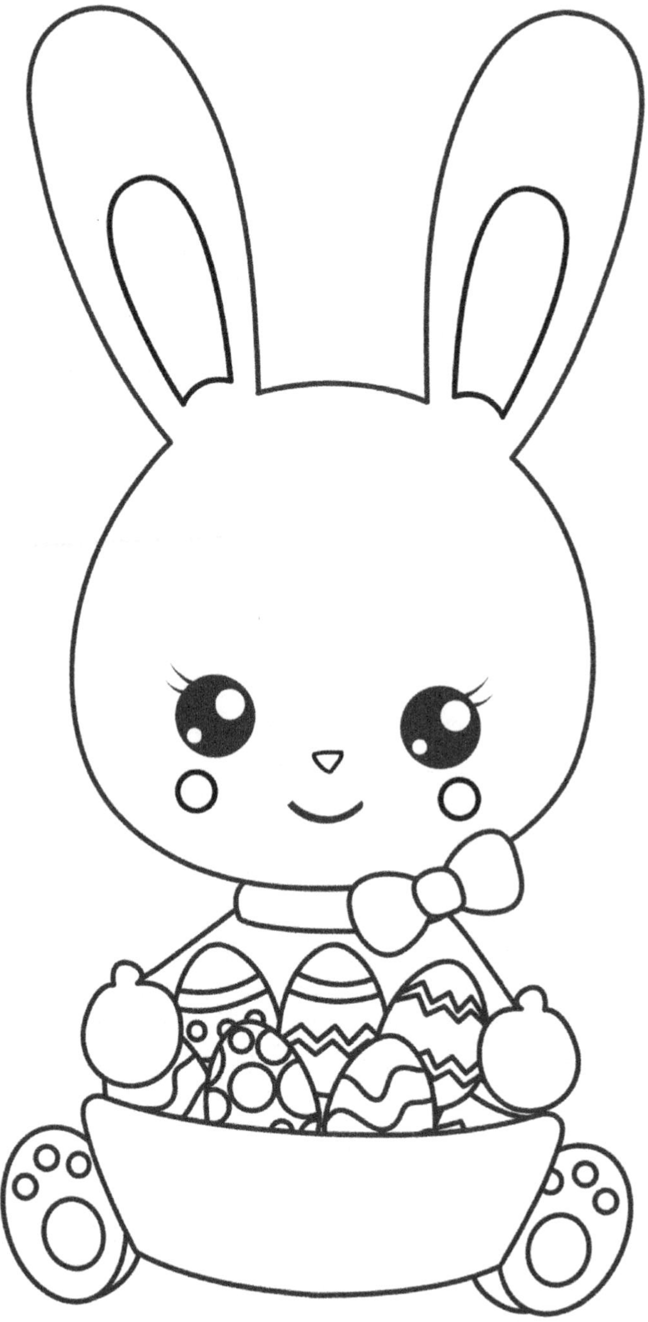

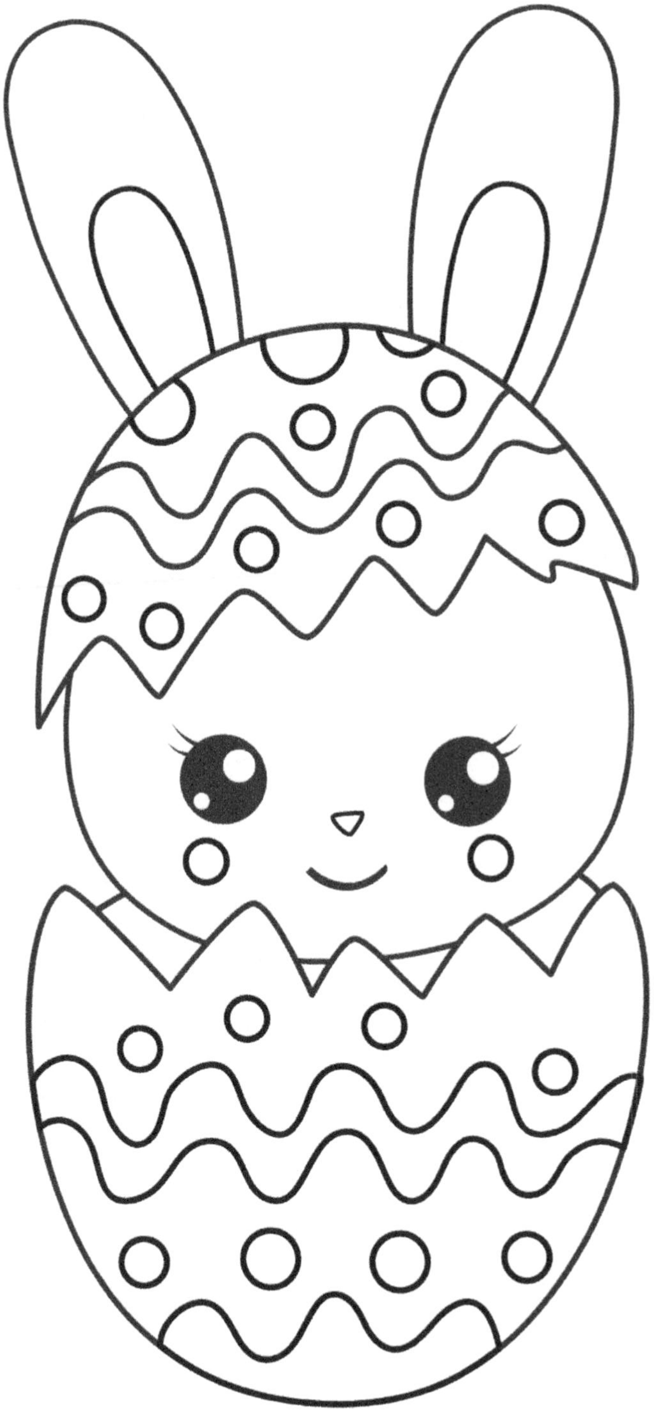

Made in the USA
Coppell, TX
02 April 2022

75916507R00057